Janeah Rose

FINDING HAPPINESS
WITHOUT CHILDREN

A Personal Journey of Trials, Tribulations, and Hope

JANEAH ROSE

Finding Happiness without Children

A Personal Journey of Trials, Tribulations, and Hope

Janeah Rose

iUniverse, Inc.
New York Bloomington

Copyright © 2010 by Janeah Rose

All rights reserved. No part of this book may be used or reproduced by any means, graphic, electronic, or mechanical, including photocopying, recording, taping or by any information storage retrieval system without the written permission of the publisher except in the case of brief quotations embodied in critical articles and reviews.

iUniverse books may be ordered through booksellers or by contacting:

iUniverse
1663 Liberty Drive
Bloomington, IN 47403
www.iuniverse.com
1-800-Authors (1-800-288-4677)

Because of the dynamic nature of the Internet, any Web addresses or links contained in this book may have changed since publication and may no longer be valid. The views expressed in this work are solely those of the author and do not necessarily reflect the views of the publisher, and the publisher hereby disclaims any responsibility for them.

ISBN: 978-1-4502-1022-5 (sc)
ISBN: 978-1-4502-1020-1 (hc)
ISBN: 978-1-4502-1021-8 (ebook)

Printed in the United States of America

iUniverse rev. date: 02/23/2010

Contents

Foreward		vii
Acknowledgments		ix
Preface		xi
Introduction		xiii
Chapter 1	A Lifelong Dream	1
Chapter 2	A Woman's Intuition	7
Chapter 3	Listening to Our Bodies	11
Chapter 4	Grieving the Loss	15
Chapter 5	Adoption Is Not for Everyone	21
Chapter 6	Leaving a Legacy Without Children	27
Chapter 7	Discovering Our Gifts	31
Chapter 8	Support Groups	33
Chapter 9	Finding Happiness in Our Choices	37
Chapter 10	The Trip of a Lifetime	45
Chapter 11	Making a Difference Without Children	49
Chapter 12	Filling the Void	55
Chapter 13	Finding Our Purpose	59
Chapter 14	Finding Strength	63
Chapter 15	Words of Wisdom	65
Chapter 16	The Voices We Hear	67
Chapter 17	Enjoy the Good Life	71
Chapter 18	Women's Views	75
Chapter 19	Not Having a Choice	77
Chapter 20	Love Thy Family	81
Chapter 21	Unconditional Love	87
Chapter 22	Finding Our Passion	91
Chapter 23	Believing in Yourself	95

Chapter 24	Overcoming Criticism	99
Chapter 25	Laughter: Still the Best Medicine	103
Chapter 26	Cherishing Our Friendships like Children	107
Chapter 27	Romance Without Children	113
Chapter 28	Letting Go of Fear	115
Chapter 29	Letting Go of Resentment	117
Chapter 30	Life Is What We Make It	119
Chapter 31	A Greater Purpose in Life	123
Chapter 32	Childless After a Loss	127
Chapter 33	Awakening to Our Healing Powers	131
Chapter 34	Feeling Complete Without Children	133
Chapter 35	Being Happy with Who We Are	135
Chapter 36	Ten Secrets to Happiness Without Children	137

Foreward

I first met Janeah many years ago. She is a gifted psychic, and both myself, family members, friends, and many of my patients saw her and received reassurance and guidance which was quite phenomenal. This book will meet a need that is not always addressed in this world. It addresses the shock, the pain, the grief, the anger and the despair of those told that they will not be able to have children. This theme resonates with many of my own experiences, but another theme flows through her story, a theme which resonated just as much, the theme of women nurturing other women.

The journey to wholeness, and to wisdom, is best taken accompanied by good friends travelling the same path, sharing stories, food, and drink, laughing, weeping, working together, and welcoming others along the way. Sometimes unlikely companions join us with their stories, and some of us take different paths, like those paths in a Celtic tree of life, with all paths are intertwined. Sometimes we are joined by children, some those to whom we have given birth, and some who have been birthed by others. Sometimes we are the midwives and doulas for others, never having the experience of birth but reaching out instinctively to be part of the joy of creation. All of us are part of each other's journey, learning from the experiences we each have and sharing our own.

Our children are gifts for us, for some cultures it is believed that the "grandmothers" spend many years in deciding who will bear these gifts into the world. However, our children are not ours; they are gifts for all to share, to love, and to nurture along the path. They bring us memories of ourselves, but they are not us. They neither define us, nor are mere extensions of us. We all have a role in nurturing them, as we journey, and we learn that we can love many children, and the most important of all, we learn that we can nurture that child within us all, with the echoes of the women who have travelled the path before us.

I do not mean to exclude those wonderful beings we call men from this path, as they too have deep yearnings for children, for companions, for good food and drink and to protect others along the path. The warriors are also "mothers" in their own way, just as mothers can be warriors. Some of us meet our own warrior, some do not. Some warriors meet us some do not. However, there is a place in the heart of all of us where there nestles the child we once were. That child who without nurturing can retreat into despair, or can bring us joy, laughter, and even more companions on our journey. Janeah's story will be a welcome companion for those who cannot meet her in person.

H. Jane Wakefield-Flint/ registered Psychologist

Acknowledgments

I am greatly thankful to my dear mother, whose enthusiasm and encouragement has meant the world to me. Her many stories and quotes from my childhood were all very important to this book, and she reminded me of many little details that I had forgotten. I'm thankful that she has such a great memory at ninety years of age.

I want to offer a special thanks to Helen, my lifelong friend who has been so supportive and encouraging as I wrote this book. I not only want to thank her for believing in me and the book contents, but also for always being there for me throughout this entire journey.

Nicole is also deserving of a special thanks for her many hours of devotion to this project. Her cover design is simply stunning.

I would also like to thank everyone for the interviews, letters, and e-mails that I share in this book. Their input has helped me tremendously in putting this book together, and their continued support is phenomenal. I will be forever indebted to all of them. I know that many of these women shared stories from a very sensitive and personal area of their lives, and for that I am especially grateful.

I want to say a special thanks to my partner, friend, and love, Keith, who stood by me, and whose words of optimism, enthusiasm, and encouragement kept me going when I faltered.

I would like to thank my friend Zoey Taylor for all her help, enthusiasm, and support.

Also deserving of a thank-you is my brother Nat, whose ideas and titles for this book kept me inspired from the very beginning. He takes the place of any kids I could have had with his love and understanding. If everyone had a brother like him, the world would be a better place.

I want to thank my friend Erin for all her hours of editing: thank you a hundred times.

A special thanks goes to Diane, whose technical support, offered via long-distance phone calls at all hours of the day and night, have been more than appreciated.

Preface

Do you have children? Do you regret not having children? Do you want children? Such simple questions! But for millions of women, these questions bring fear, anxiety, depression, and marital conflict—to name only a few.

My husband and I struggled for many years with infertility, and just when we thought a new door would open, we were faced with another door closing: a series of marital conflicts and disagreements that ultimately led to the breakdown of our marriage.

Luckily, I had a very supportive family, as well as many friends. Nonetheless, infertility was a devastating experience that I wouldn't wish on anyone.

Because of my own experiences and the dilemma it brought to me, I wanted to write this book for all the women who may also be fearful of their future without children, struggling to cope in a fertile world that seems to have left them behind.

This book aims to help childless women understand the myriad of feelings and emotions they may experience. It will also provide some unique ways to cope with holidays, manage family relationships, maintain physical health, and monitor well-being. It also provides a look into other childless women's lives, offering the secrets of how they found happiness without children.

There are no absolutes when it comes to childlessness; although most women endure the same social stigma, we all seem to find our own personal way to heal and grow from this fate.

You will find that this book offers enlightenment, inspiration, and hope. It encourages all childless women to awaken to their higher selves and triumph through their hardships.

In order to protect their identities, the names and other characteristics of the women whose stories have been printed throughout the chapters of this book have been changed.

The information, ideas, and suggestions throughout this book are not intended as a substitute for professional advice. Before following any suggestions contained in this book, please consult your personal physician or mental-health professional. Neither the author nor the publisher shall be liable or responsible for any loss or damage allegedly arising as a consequence of your use or application of any information or suggestions in this book.

Introduction

Stories always seem to flow with the pace of the comb while a woman sits beneath a cape in a stylist's chair. Many companionships and friendships begin in the salon, a place full of laughter, jokes, gossip, and sometimes even tears. When I started working in a well-known beauty salon in the 1970s, I was barely out of high school—eighteen years old, determined, and somewhat naïve, but with a great sense of humor that could usually help me see the brighter side of things.

However, at times, even my sense of humor could not bring the slightest hint of laughter to a woman who was tormented with a dilemma. On these occasions, serious conversations would arise with women who feared getting old because they were without children—not by choice, but by chance. This topic always seemed to take precedence over topics such as love affairs, cheating partners, new romances, the latest movies or fashions. This topic also seemed to stir up some very personal stories among perfect strangers; their willingness to share such intimate experiences always amazed me. I loved it because the client no longer was paying any attention to how I was styling her head of hair, and I would get paid to listen to these interesting stories.

At the time, I didn't think menopause, infertility, or childlessness would ever affect me, so I really didn't give the subject too much thought. I remember these ladies to be in their midthirties to midforties, which at the time seemed ancient. They were mostly career oriented; they had nice cars, beautiful dream homes, and husbands who spoiled them rotten. I was always under the impression that they were happy, because they seemed to have everything—until one day, one of these clients commented that she hoped she would not live a long life. I did not often find myself at a loss for words, but this was one of those times. Finally, I managed to ask why. Her answer baffled me even more. With sadness in her voice, she said, "Because I don't want to be old and all alone in the world."

This was one of those times when I knew my humor would not be appreciated, so I quickly responded, "Well, if I'm still alive, I will come and visit you!"

Little did I know that one day, I would be walking in their shoes, facing my own life without children. When I found myself in their situation, I suddenly remembered how their feelings and emotions: sadness, loneliness, alienation, guilt, fear, depression, and so on. Not only could I suddenly relate to those feelings, but I was actually living them. This worried me more than anything, because I remembered those women's sad faces and how they sat in my chair and described life without children as though it were a curse or punishment for something they had done.

I felt for certain that I was going to be on the same path of heartache and fear of the future, because it wasn't long before all of my friends and sisters were getting married and having kids like clockwork. I became an auntie to a growing group of little kids faster than I could say, "It's a girl!" or "It's a boy!" As the most sought-after babysitter in the entire neighborhood, I was soon an expert at changing dirty diapers, heating up bottles, and telling bedtime stories. This daily routine made it even more evident just how much I really loved and needed kids in my life. I felt somehow cheated, and I knew my life was going to be a long and lonely road if I had to live it without kids.

I remember being so humiliated every time I was asked, "When are you going to start your family?" I always tried to think of the simplest and politest way to give them a straightforward answer without the embarrassment. Unfortunately, there really was no other answer except the sad and simple truth, which was, "I can't have my own children." Believe it or not, the next question was usually even more thoughtless and came with no hesitation: "Why not?" I almost said many times, "What business is it of yours?"

I often think back to all those poor women in the seventies who were telling me of their heartaches and personal situations. How difficult life must have been for them back in those days, when life coaches, therapists, support groups, and self-help books were almost unheard-of. Times have certainly changed for the better; nowadays, Web sites and self-help books offer assistance for just about every issue, and help seems to be readily available for everyone. Educational materials on everything from infertility to abortions are widely accessible.

Many times throughout my own struggles, I wanted more than anything to ask those former clients of mine whether all those feelings of discontentment, fear, anxiety, discouragement, and heartache ever went away. How long had it taken them to find contentment, inner peace, and happiness? Where had their journey without children taken them? How had they found their purpose in life? Were all childless women destined to secretly face this journey alone?

So many unanswered questions surrounded the stigma and heartache of my infertility. I desperately needed answers from women who had actually been there, who had actually journeyed to happiness in those same shoes. From the time I had my surgery and learned of my fate, I embarked on a secret mission to find out just how these women had found their true happiness without children. I not only felt a strong need to learn how to be one of these women, but I also wanted to share these secrets with every childless woman in the world. I had to find out just exactly what women who were childless by chance were doing to make themselves feel whole and complete. I knew I wasn't alone, and I needed more than ever to talk to these women in person. I had so many questions for them; I needed to feel their emotions and get their feedback on life as a childless woman. I guess I just needed to know for certain, deep down in my heart, that there really was hope of happiness without children.

I know one thing for sure: it is much harder to go through a hysterectomy as a childless woman suffering a life-or-death medical emergency than it is to choose a hysterectomy as a course of treatment for other ailments when you already have children. Then again, no matter what the reason is for a hysterectomy at any age, the prospect of such a surgery still leaves a woman facing a sudden, life-changing dilemma that carries many risk factors.

Luckily for me, I was able to set up my own beauty salon in my own home, where I would once again have the golden opportunity of talking with and listening to my clients, just like old times. What could be better therapy than styling women's hair—something I loved—while enjoying the privilege and honor of talking to women all day long on just about any topic imaginable? The salon always seemed to be offer the perfect time and place for a serious talk, without interruptions. I soon discovered that not much had changed in the hair-styling world: it was never long before the topic of children was in the air, and I connected with an amazing number of women who were going through exactly the same emotions as I was over being childless.

I've been passionate about writing a book like this for more than twenty years, but surprising as it may seem, only during the last year or so have I actually sat down and gotten serious about it. Little omens were starting to pop up everywhere; for instance, every time I looked for some odd or end in an old trunk, I seemed to run across the torn and tattered pages of the old journals I had kept for over ten years. In addition, dozens of little articles from magazines and newspapers were suddenly falling out of their unusual places. Everywhere I turned, books and magazines regaled me with tales of women who found their purpose or wrote their first books at fifty. As the signs added up, I felt that it really was the right time to quit procrastinating.

I started by sending out e-mails to some of my friends, acquaintances, relatives, and clients who were also childless, telling them what I was going to be writing about and asking whether they would be interested in sharing their stories of how childlessness had affected their lives. Because I have twenty-five friends who don't have kids, it was easy for me to gather firsthand accounts. I also started telling everyone I met what I was going to be writing about, and the response from total strangers was overwhelming. I received more stories than I had ever hoped to get, and I heard many heartbreaking stories that would be good movie material. I'm still receiving nice letters and cards on the subject to this day, which I truly appreciate.

Not long after I requested these stories, the first letter I received from a childless woman inspired me to write this story of how infertility has changed women's lives.

Chapter 1
A Lifelong Dream

Thinking back to my early childhood, I would say that my motherly instincts awakened when I was only around seven or eight years of age. What little girl doesn't dream of being a mommy someday? I grew up on the southern coast of British Columbia, where I was big sister, babysitter, and caregiver to my four younger siblings: two brothers and two sisters.

I was kind of a free-spirited child, with a mind of my own; I often rebelled against my strict Roman Catholic Italian upbringing. I really was the child who gave my parents the most worry. From the time I was two years old, I apparently would climb out of my crib and wander outside, looking for my dad at his workplace. More than once, the police would pick me up many hours later, several blocks away from my home—a luckily unharmed toddler who was just looking for her dad. Apparently, I was always inquisitive about everything and had to get a logical answer for everything that intrigued me, or I would just keep asking questions: "Where do babies come from?" "Why is the sky blue?" If I didn't get the answer I was looking for, I would ask someone else, whether it was a neighbor or a perfect stranger walking down the street. I wouldn't quit asking the question until I felt satisfied with the answer.

From the time I was five years old, I loved to play house. I would dress up in my mom's clothes and high heels and pretend

I was the mom of all my dolls or of my baby brother. Everywhere I went, I had to tote a baby doll in my arms or push one around in a little buggy. As if it happened yesterday, I can still clearly remember painstakingly changing my dolls' real diapers with real safety pins. I was often caught putting my six-month-old brother into my doll buggy; when I wanted him out, I would tip the buggy over like a wheelbarrow and pick him up as if he were one of my dolls. From the time I was three years old, all I ever wanted was dolls—not just at Christmas or on birthdays, but anytime. Mom said I was just plain "baby crazy" and told everyone that when I grew up, I would most likely have at least six or seven kids.

I remember getting one of my last dolls at eleven years of age, if you can imagine—I've heard of girls that age having real babies.

At that particular time, my baby sister had just come into the world. My mom taught me very quickly how to change a real dirty diaper, how to mix formula, and how to fill a real baby bottle. I also learned very quickly how to bathe and handle a tiny little newborn without injuring the soft spot on top of her head. Mom thought that if she let me do a lot of the motherly things she usually did, I would be a pro at it by the time I had my own children. Around this time, I began yearning for my own babies; I wanted to be a mom more than anything. I completely took over the role of mother to my new baby sister.

That same year, the walking dolls came into existence. Mom knew how much I loved dolls of any description, so she thought she would surprise me with one last doll for my collection. It was often a toss-up as to which one I would want to play with: my nice, new doll who always stayed quiet and pretty, or the real baby who needed changing and feeding. Regardless, my new doll was special to me, especially after I learned that Mom had saved all her extra pennies from the grocery money so that she would have enough money saved up by Christmas. This big, beautiful, blonde, blue-eyed doll stood beside my bed until I left home at eighteen, when I graciously left it behind for my baby sister, telling her to take good care of her because I wanted to pass the doll down to my little girl one day.

By the time I turned eighteen, most of my girlfriends were dating or had steady boyfriends. One of my friends had already had a child, so everyone got lots of hands-on experience with nurturing and caring for a baby at a very early age. This experience only confirmed that all I wanted more than anything was to have a baby of my own. Needless to say, our lives were changing at a fast and furious pace. Education was no longer our first priority; when we got together, all we ever talked about was boys, weddings, and babies. We never discussed careers, colleges, or fancy cars. Anyone eavesdropping would have heard statements like "When I have kids, I will be strict," and "When I have my kids, I hope they look like me." Never in the conversation would anyone ever hear the words "If I ever have kids." It was just taken for granted that when we got married, the first priority would be to have a baby.

I was a dreamer from the time I was six years old. I would wake up and tell my parents in graphic detail just exactly what my dreams were all about. I apparently never had a nightmare, only very realistic, vivid dreams—dreams that I would describe with as much detail as a three-hour movie, recounting every color and object as though I had been there only minutes before.

My girlfriends and I always talked about our dreams as if they were our itinerary for the future. We dreamed of the men we wanted to marry, what kind of wedding we wanted, how many kids we were going to have, and what sex we hoped our kids would be. Kids were always a big part of my dreams and conversations from as far back as I can remember.

When I was eighteen, I brought home my first serious boyfriend—the one who actually asked my dad for my hand in marriage. We fell in love at first sight and had lots of fun together. Everyone was happy for us when we announced our engagement; they thought we were the perfect couple. Our parents made wedding plans with us, and everything seemed to be just like a dream.

Unfortunately, one very important ingredient was missing in the man I thought was Mr. Right. Just weeks before the big day, my fiancé announced to me that he had no interest whatsoever in having children. Heartbroken beyond words, I broke off the engagement and canceled all the wedding plans. It was one of the hardest things I ever had to do: make the choice between love or children. As hard as it was, I decided to wait until I could have both. I got a lot of criticism over the fact that I had broken up with such a nice guy just because he didn't want children. However, my dream of parenthood was one of the main reasons I wanted to get married in the first place, so there would be no point in tying the knot if we weren't going to have children, even if I was in love with him.

I daydreamed about getting married and having kids from the time I was very young. Because of that passion, I ended up getting engaged several times before ever getting married. I felt that my life wasn't going to be complete unless I got married and had kids of my own. Unfortunately, my fiancés either didn't want kids or weren't crazy about kids as I was, so I ended the engagements with little or no regrets. I never looked back on what could have been; I just thought that sooner or later, I would meet someone who loved and wanted kids as much as I did. I never gave up hope of finding that man; it was just a matter of believing that I would—and having the patience to wait.

After cautiously and patiently waiting for almost seven years, I finally met and fell in love with the man I had always dreamed of. I was twenty-five years old at the time, and I married him three months later, just before my twenty-sixth birthday. We had a quaint little wedding in the middle of December in the Okanagan Valley of British Columbia. It was just like a fairy tale; big, white, fluffy snowflakes gently fell and covered the ground, which made everything feel even more magical and romantic. My father proudly gave me away to his new son-in-law, whom he felt was the perfect man for his number-one daughter. I truly felt like a princess wearing the gorgeous, white satin wedding dress that my mother had worn thirty years earlier, when she married my father.

We weren't married long before we started to plan for our life with a child or children. We bought an acre of land and built a huge house with five bedrooms, just in case we had a big family. It seemed I was constantly surrounded by little children, either cutting their hair or babysitting them. Most of our friends had two or more, so I babysat a great deal in my home whenever I had the time or opportunity. I found that arrangement to be perfect; I never ever tired of their constant demands and or the responsibility. If anything, my babysitting experiences only confirmed that my love for kids was genuine and wasn't about to change anytime soon. I also knew that I had to have at least one child in my own life in order to feel complete.

We were married only a year when friends began asking the inevitable questions: "Are you guys going to have kids?" "When are you guys going to start your family?" We always said yes to the first question without hesitation and always answered the second question with, "Hopefully soon."

I continued babysitting on a daily basis and worked with my clients to fit appointments into the kids' schedule. Wherever I went, the kids went with me; car seats, cuddle seats, baby bottles, and teddy bears became fixtures around my busy household. The funny thing was that it felt so natural to play part-time mom to all the kids. I loved everything about having the kids around me, except when people would ask, "What's your little girl's name?" or "How old is your daughter?" I hated to explain that they were not mine, because then the next question would always be, "How come you don't have any kids of your own?" It was a question I was beginning to wonder about myself.

Another two years passed, and I was still only a babysitter and an auntie several times over—I was still not a mom or even displaying any signs of becoming one. Don't get me wrong: The babysitting was great, and I loved the kids dearly, but they weren't mine. At the end of the day, they had their coats on to run into their parents' arms. From the minute their mother walked in the door, you heard, "Mommy, Mommy!"

There was no denying it: by this time, I was getting desperate. My next plan of action was the questionable fertility drug. I was ready to try almost anything, and drugs seemed the most accessible.

I knew there would be the chance of multiple births, but at the time, I didn't care if I had six at a time. I just wanted to conceive a child, and if I conceived more than one, so be it. I would just have to buy two of everything—or three or four. People said things like, "Are you crazy?" or "Do you realize that you could die giving birth to a litter of kids?"

I ignored all of these negative remarks until I actually sat down with the doctor for a heart-to-heart talk on the reality of the drug treatment. He said, "I can give you the drug, all right, but you will have to go home and build a litter box."

I smiled at his humor and said, "What if I take a smaller dose? Will I have a better chance of having only one?"

He smiled as he looked over the top of his glasses and said, "I can't guarantee that, my dear, but that is a good question—and one I've never been asked before."

My husband and I walked out of the office without saying a word, but both of us knew that a round of fertility drugs were no longer an option, only a door that closed in front of our eyes.

Chapter 2
A Woman's Intuition

As time went marching by, my husband and I became very discouraged. All of our friends and family members were busy having children, and the more I saw their babies, the more I wanted one of my own.

Decorating the baby's room was becoming even more of a priority than getting pregnant. One day, while I was shopping for a shower gift for a girlfriend who was having her first child, I stumbled across the cutest little white baby crib. I thought that it would be perfect for our baby, and that I may as well get started with the baby room that I had been contemplating. Without giving it another thought, I very proudly took it home as if I already had a baby to put in it. I worked around this little white crib for the design of the baby's room for the next several months, spending endless amounts of time and money on everything that a baby would ever need or want.

I would often get asked, "What's with the little white baby crib?"

I would always just answer with, "It's for when we have a baby." I would never answer this statement with, "It's for if I ever have a baby." I always for some reason talked as though the baby would be in my arms any day. I always believed that if you wanted something badly enough, and you visualized it, you could manifest it. I practiced this visualization on a daily basis, especially while mixing baby formulas, changing diapers, and rocking a baby to sleep in my arms. I thought that the quality time I spent with these children whom I loved like my own would offer the perfect opportunity for my visualization of true motherhood.

My mother continued knitting baby blankets and stuffed toys for the grandchild she prayed her oldest daughter would have. My friends would always give me pointers on how to change a diaper and how to hold an infant properly. It was always, "Here, let me show you how to hold a baby." I usually had more experience than the young mother telling me.

I was beginning to get innocent comments like, "You will make such a good mom one day, because you love kids so much." I babysat more nieces, nephews, and children of friends or neighbors, until it looked as if I were running a day-care facility on any given day. Broken crayons, coloring books, teddy bears, and toys were always strewn across my floor, along with baby bottles and pacifiers that had been left behind as the kids were being rushed off by their parents at five o'clock every day.

Whenever anyone entered our home for the first time, they would always ask, "How many kids do you have?" or comment that I must be a busy mother.

My usual response was, "I wish."

Another two years went by, and I was beginning to feel as if I were chasing an impossible dream. I was still not pregnant—still only a babysitter. I began to have these visions of myself as a childless woman who would be alone all of her life. I tried to ignore them and tell myself that they were only a result of the stress of trying to conceive a child, or that I was overreacting. However these visions were becoming more and more real. I would often wake up in the night after having a dream of an empty little white crib. This, I knew, was not a good sign. I also knew that a woman's intuition is very real, and that most women have this intuition, or inner voice. I knew I had it, and I also felt that this particular intuition was not about to go away. It was going to be life-changing, so I was not about to ignore it.

My dear friends were very supportive and were always there to listen, although I never told them about my intuition. Often, a conversation would lead to the words that I didn't want to hear: "Kids aren't everything," or "You have a great husband," and "It's not the end of the world if you don't have kids." Unwilling to hear those words and unwilling to give in to my visions and dreams, I would very politely change the subject. I didn't realize then that those dear friends were only trying to support and comfort me in the only way they knew how. Looking back now, I see more truth in those comforting words than I recognized at the time.

My intuitive visions were making it hard to stay positive and focused. This little voice inside me kept saying, "You'll never be a mom," and "You will be a childless woman." My fears were beginning to interfere with my everyday life. I spent many hours fretting over the fact that I could end up childless, living a life without children. Consequently, I wasn't able to visualize anything positive at that point. That worried me the most, as I had always been able to think positive and see the good in every scenario, no matter how bleak it looked at the time.

I had landscaped a beautiful flower garden to get my mind off kids, pregnancy, and the strain that infertility was placing on my marriage. I loved designing and working tirelessly, day after day, in this little piece of paradise. When it was all in colorful bloom, it looked like something from *Better Homes and Gardens*. But at this particular time in my life, I couldn't even get motivated enough to water it, let alone find time to sit and enjoy it. I couldn't get excited about anything. Subconsciously, I was somewhere else, far away, wondering what my life would be like if I did not become a mom.

I knew that it wasn't like me to be so negative and distant with everyone. I had always looked at the bright side of things, no matter how grim and dark they seemed. I had to take a step back and ask myself, "What is the lesson in this? Why can't I just accept the fact that I may be childless?" I would always ask myself, "Am I being punished? Why isn't God answering my prayers?"

Waiting to get pregnant was very stressful; every month, I would think "Maybe this month," and get my hopes up. Of course, when the end of the month arrived and I once again saw that I was not pregnant, the disappointment would happen all over again. That process would be hard on any marriage, I'm sure.

More and more, I would find myself in a meditative state and then wake up feeling as though I had been somewhere else. It could happen anywhere. For example, I could drive to a destination and then wonder how I had gotten there, because I didn't remember driving through the roads that had taken me there. This happened on more than one occasion. I would be off somewhere else, far away, and for some strange reason, I kept seeing myself in a bed, wearing a white hospital gown. I couldn't see why I was there—only that I was there, and that I was upset, because it was not the maternity ward. I felt that I would be all right, but I still wasn't happy about the vision.

This went on for several weeks until I very secretly made an appointment with my doctor to see what was really wrong. I always listened to my inner voice, as well as my body. I trusted my body and my visions, because they had always been right in the past. I knew this was no exception. Some women called it their gut feeling; some called it their premonition; others called it their instincts. I called it a woman's intuition.

My advice for women who want to stay healthy is this: Be your own advocate! Listen to your own body, and see your physician on a regular basis. Last, but certainly not least, trust your intuition, especially if you feel that something is wrong.

Following your instincts can save your life. Following my instincts saved mine.

Chapter 3
Listening To Our Bodies

I never told anyone about my intuitive vision of myself in a hospital bed; it was as though I were carrying a secret. I just knew that something was wrong with me, and I wanted to take care of it as soon as possible. I had a pap test and several blood tests done immediately, and sure enough, the results that I had foreseen for many weeks were no longer just a vision. They were very real, very devastating, and tremendously shocking, to say the least.

I will never forget that fateful Friday afternoon. At times, it seems like yesterday, and at other times, I can hardly believe it happened at all. I had been picking raspberries in the garden for the raspberry juice that I made every summer, and when I came into the house after a few hours of working, I happened to glance at the answering machine. I had missed a call. My heart pounded as I took a deep breath and sat down to listen carefully. I knew as soon as I pressed the Play button that the message was going to be from the doctor's office, and it was going to tell me the news that I had subconsciously been waiting to hear for months—the news that I knew would ultimately change my life forever.

The message was very short and to the point: "The doctor would like you to come in as soon as possible to go over your test results. Our office will be closed for the long weekend but will reopen on Monday."

The next three days were the longest days of my life, as one can imagine. I didn't want to start imagining negative outcomes or even talk to anyone who might be negative; my prayers at that time were only that I would be healthy and would live for a long time to come. Later, I would be awed to realize that in all my prayers that weekend, I never once prayed for kids—rather strange for someone who thought that kids were everything. I wondered if this was a clue to a bigger picture.

By Monday morning, after a sleepless night, the words "I have good news, and I have bad news" didn't exactly come as a shock.

I was scared of the bad news, so I asked, "Could you please give me the good news first?"

He said, "Fortunately, all you need is a hysterectomy." He seemed to be somewhat hesitant about the bad news, but I felt as though he had already given me the bad news. When I heard the word "hysterectomy," I knew that I would never be able to have a baby. He continued, "Hysterectomies are performed by the millions every year. They are not serious, and you will be fine."

I said, "This news of not being able to have a baby is the bad news for me, but what do *you* call the bad news?"

With the saddest look on his face, and one I will never forget, he said, "The bad news, unfortunately, is that you have what is called cervical cancer, and if it doesn't get treated immediately, it will be invasive."

Dumbfounded and in a state of shock, all I could think of to say was, "How bad is it? Can I think about this for a week or so?"

He answered without hesitation. "I'm sorry, but no. I want to operate as soon as possible—like this weekend."

I couldn't believe what I was hearing; it seemed unreal, like a bad dream I wanted to wake up from. I knew in my heart, though, that this was serious business, and I didn't have time to waste thinking about anything. So I replied with, "I guess you'd better book my surgery and get it over with."

With that, he put his arm around me and said, "I know how much you really wanted to have children, but believe me, dear, this is your only route to take." I could tell by the sadness in his soft voice and the tear in his eyes that if there were any way he could have changed my fate, he would have.

Despite my watery eyes and foggy head, I found my way back to the car in the pouring rain. With drenched hands and soaking-wet hair, I fumbled with the keys, trying to open the car door. When I looked inside the window, I realized why the door wouldn't open: it wasn't even my car. By this time, I realized that the nurse had been right: I really wasn't in any shape to drive home alone. After finding and getting into my car, I sat there for the longest time, just watching the pouring rain pound down on the windshield, not wanting to go anywhere.

I felt this pain and anger building up inside of me: pain from knowing that my lifelong dream had just been stripped away from me, and anger from knowing that I couldn't do anything about it. The idea of cancer didn't seem to bother me as much as thoughts of surgery, going under anesthesia, and not being able to have a child.

I'll never know how I made it home that day; my mind was a million miles away. I kept hearing the doctor's voice saying, "You have cancer." But as soon as I thought about those words for a few seconds, my mind jumped right back to the reality that I was not going to have children. That, to me, was the worst shock of all, because my intuition told me that I would be fine with the cancer—that it would not take my life. But it also kept saying, "You were right; you are not going to be a mom."

I tried to be realistic about the whole traumatic incident. I had to get prepared to have surgery that weekend—not for tonsillitis or appendicitis, but for something much more serious. When the doctor had first given me the news, it hit me hard, as it would anyone—after all, I'm only human. But at the same time, I was mad at God not for giving me cancer, but for not allowing me to have children. I wondered what I had done in my life to deserve this. I always went to church and prayed and was a devout Catholic. I was very confused, and nothing seemed to make much sense.

I thanked God for not allowing the cancer to go farther and take my life. But I was still mad at Him for not allowing me to have even one child. It just didn't make any sense to me. I began to think about how some women could have babies at the drop of a hat, and some babies were born by accident, and some babies were just left on a stranger's doorstep. I kept thinking, over and over again, of how unfair it was that I couldn't have even one.

The only thing that did make any kind of sense to me then and now was the importance of listening to my body and how I needed to be my own advocate. Had I not listened, I would not be here today, writing this book.

Chapter 4
Grieving The Loss

When I was brought to my room at the hospital, and I got into the nice, fresh, white bed that was waiting for me, it was like déjà vu. I could hardly believe it myself: everything was just as I had seen it in my vision.

The surgery went well, and I came out of it with flying colors, just as the doctor had predicted. But from the time I could sit up and wash my face, I kept crying. I couldn't seem to get past the fact that I was thirty-five, childless, and in sudden menopause. As I lay in that bed for the duration of the week, different questions went through my mind, such as, "Will I feel as good physically? Will I feel like my clients in the seventies, who were childless and lonely and fearful of getting old? Will I feel complete as a woman now that I don't have female organs?"

I must have had every nurse on the floor wanting a quick intuitive reading into their future after they heard that I had had the intuition that something was wrong. I loved the nurses, because they all treated me like royalty. They were always buzzing all around me, making sure I had everything I needed to make me comfortable. The funny thing was that I wasn't sick. I felt great; it was just my mind that was in turmoil. I was still in shock and disbelief about being left childless. One night, when the nurse came to take my temperature, I remember telling her that I was going to go on a mission to invent a pill to grow another uterus.

Not long after the surgery, other questions popped up in my head. Would I ever measure up to women who had children? Would my marriage ever be the same with no children? How could I live a happy life without children? What would my purpose be? I had always been a fanatic about kids. I had all these dreams of being a mother of a big family—like my own mom, who had seven children. I began to wonder just what else was there in life besides children. What would I have to look forward to? Why did I feel as though I had lost something I had never had? I remember asking myself why God had not answered my prayers. I had always gotten the impression that if I was good, and if I prayed long and hard for something, I would get whatever it was I had been praying for. I wondered if there was any point to praying for anything anymore.

I felt empty, lonely, and very much cheated out of my childbearing life. I suppose a lot of these feelings were exaggerated, because everything had happened so terribly fast, with no time to really think about the effects of the surgery itself, such as all of the menopausal symptoms. Feelings of being incomplete as a woman were slowly surfacing, and I didn't know who to blame or where to run. I just felt like pulling the blankets up over my face and staying in bed forever. Thoughts of regret filtered through my mind. Should I have waited to get pregnant before having the surgery? Would I have a happy marriage without kids? Thoughts like this gnawed constantly at my brain, sometimes making it difficult to focus on anything else.

I had to keep reminding myself that God hadn't given me a disease that would take my life. I thanked Him every day for that—and for giving me the power of my intuition! That intuition had saved my life. I felt for certain that I had a guardian angel looking out for me.

As thankful as I was for all these things, I still felt alone, scared, and full of questions that seemed to haunt my every thought. I asked myself the same questions every day: Would

I ever be happy again? Why had this happened to me? Where would I find love and happiness, if not with children?

When I would think about my life without children, which was constantly, I would almost feel sick to my stomach, particularly when I saw a mom with a newborn baby, or when I saw a pregnant woman or a baby in a commercial on television. I would go into a very depressed state—filled with resentment, anger, and even jealousy. I would actually be very jealous of girls who were having babies, if you can believe that; I had never ever been jealous of anyone or anything in my life. I stayed away from the mall, which seemed full of mothers and babies, pregnant women, or kids getting their pictures taken with Santa.

After many months of crying and feeling sorry for myself, which was all part of the grieving process, I thought that I had better start picking up all the missing pieces of my life. If I didn't figure out my life soon, I was going to drive myself crazy. I was glad I had cried as much as I had, because crying really wasn't something that I had done a lot of in my childhood, but I had cried enough to make up for my whole childhood and then some. These were healing tears for me, because it always felt better to cry than to keep all the emotions inside.

I wondered if all women who were suddenly faced with being childless felt the same way. My mission at that point was to get involved with women who were also childless by chance. I wanted to ask them how they had overcome the stigma and how long it had taken them to grieve, so that I could determine where I was in the process and prepare myself for any other hurdles I might face.

I began to search for answers; I needed to know that I wasn't alone. I got in touch with everyone and anyone I knew who were without children. I went to the library and bookstores and read up on everything about menopause and childlessness. I was surprised at how many of my friends and acquaintances were childless— mostly from early hysterectomies. It helped me to realize that I wasn't alone, and that grieving was definitely a natural part of the process. As one of those women said, "It's very similar to losing a baby."

Apart from not being able to bear children, I had lost a very important part of my body. The uterus symbolizes a woman's ability to have children; for many, it represents the essence of being a woman. Quite often after a hysterectomy, a woman feels incomplete or as if she is no longer female; these feelings stem from the loss of her pregnancy hopes and the cessation of her menstrual cycle.

I did a lot of homework on hysterectomies and the side effects women suffer afterward. I wanted to prepare myself for all the health issues that I would face down the road. My own doctor had given me the heads-up on the hot flashes, mood swings, insomnia, depression, decrease in bone mass, greater risk of osteoporosis, increased risk of cardiovascular disease, and increased possibility of urinary incontinence. At the time, the statistics for hysterectomies in North America were in the neighborhood of 550,000 per year, and it was also noted that the average age for premenopausal women having a hysterectomy in the United States was thirty-five. This made me feel a little better, since I was thirty-five when I had mine.

The hysterectomy itself is performed as the course of treatment for a number of conditions, such as cancer of the uterus or cervix, severe endometriosis, extensive fibroid tumors, uncontrolled infections, or severe hemorrhaging.

As I looked around for others who had suffered my plight, it didn't take me long to count up twenty-five friends who were childless—and more than half of whom were excited about getting together. These women had become childless by chance and had gotten over their grief. They were socially connected, career-oriented, and happy with their busy lives without children. We connected for coffee and gathered for social events as often as we could between work schedules, travel itineraries, and quality time with spouses. We formed our own little support groups, turning our homes into relaxing little retreats for meditation,

Reiki (a hands-on healing technique), and talks on women's issues every week. It was fun, interesting, and rewarding, as well as healing and educational.

Support groups are the answer for anyone who wants to spend time talking with others who have had similar experiences. Grieving after a hysterectomy is important, especially if you are a woman who always wanted children. Support is equally important for women who want to move forward, find their purpose, and carry on with a happy, healthy, and meaningful lifestyle without children. Anyone can form a group of family members, friends, and acquaintances, as long as everyone is supportive, nonjudgmental, and demonstrating a need to heal from any situation out of their control. Talking is the best form of therapy. Listening is the greatest gift anyone can have. As an even bigger gift, those who have healed can share their knowledge with others who need the support.

Talking to positive women on the subject of infertility and being childless by chance is an awesome experience. First and foremost, it helped me realize that I am not alone by any stretch of the imagination. In fact, so many women out there are willing and able to share their experiences with other childless women. It is so comforting to hear such unique and positive stories from each and every one of them and to know that they have all found a greater purpose and happy life without children.

One of these special stories is that of a thirty-eight-year-old woman I met while at a convention for Xango, a nutritious beverage, in Las Vegas. She was in her own group, called Response. We shared the same table for dinner and felt as though we had known each other all our lives.

The first thing I commented on was the beautiful outfit she was wearing, which was the same bright blue as her eyes. Then I said, "I love your perfume—it reminds me of the tropical island of Kauai."

She said, "You have great sense of smell, because that is exactly where I found the perfume—it's called Plumeria."

"I love it," I repeated, taking another whiff of it.

Before our five-course meal was served in the gorgeous dining room (where everything seemed to be pink, from the tablecloths to the plates), this lovely, soft-spoken woman introduced herself as June.

As we got to know one another, she asked, "Do you have children?"

I answered with, "No, I don't have any children. Do you?"

Her answer was touching and encouraging: "I never ever had the desire to give birth to a child, but I found that my purpose in life was to give something back, because I don't have them."

"How interesting. What, exactly, do you do to give back?"

"I do many things, but the main one is that I have four adopted children from Africa that I support financially. They give you so much gratitude—they love you and keep in touch with you. When you see how much your money does for them and how it helps them get medical and dental care, it does your heart good. It is what I recommend for everyone, especially childless women who want to feel they are loved by a child, even though they are not your own. If you want to give back and feel as if you have a purpose in life, it will fulfill all of those needs and then some."

"Thanks for sharing that advice," I told her. "I will definitely think about that and pass it on."

Chapter 5
Adoption Is Not For Everyone

Trying to get your life back on track is not always easy. Many women get discouraged, disillusioned, and very depressed. These are natural emotions that can sometimes be overwhelming.

I seemed to get angry at the drop of a hat; this apparently was all quite the norm. I would find myself crying about anything and everything, from a sad movie to a happy ending—even several years after my surgery. I couldn't sleep more than two hours on any given night, and I lost interest in everything, even myself. Moving forward was the biggest challenge, because I knew I had to rough it alone, in my own time, and in my own way.

The hardest part for me was parting with the many treasured baby things waiting in the baby room, like the little white baby crib that I had had so many dreams for. I think I loved that crib so much because it reminded me of my childhood, when all I did was take care of babies and dolls. Mostly, though, it held all the hopes and dreams of having a firstborn to tuck in at night. It was also home to many colorful, handmade baby blankets and clothes, along with knitted little bears that were gifts from friends and family. Treasured teddy bears and toys had been passed down to me for my firstborn. Anyone looking into the little room at the end of my hallway had always assumed that a baby was about to arrive any day. Cleaning out that room would be my biggest hurdle, because it meant giving up a dream.

One day, while having my hair styled, I got talking to the woman in the chair beside me. I was telling her how busy I was cleaning out a baby's room, how I didn't know what to do with all the beautiful new baby paraphernalia, and what a sad task it was.

I guess I should have known that her question was going to be, "How old are your kids?"

I didn't quite know how to tell her that I didn't have any, so I very politely said, "Actually, we can't have children."

It caught her off guard, but her answer was simple and to the point. Excitedly, she said, "Don't get rid of the baby things—do what we did! I had to fill my life with someone to care for, other than just my husband and our ten-year-old border collie. So we adopted two children, and it has completed our life in so many ways. Don't get rid of a thing until you think about adoption!"

Before I had time to comment, this friendly woman was whisked away by the stylist, but said quickly before going around the corner, "If you're wanting to have a child and can't have one of your own, I recommend adoption. Don't get rid of the baby's room. Adopting children will make your life complete!"

I never got to ask her any more questions, but her words did give me food for thought. I drove home that day with more than just a new hairstyle. I went home with a wonderful new idea— one that had never been thought about, and one that sounded marvelous. As I drove home, my thoughts were a million miles away, as usual. If we adopted a child, maybe it would make our lives complete—and hopefully a lot happier. Maybe adoption was the way to go!

Before going home that day, I decided do some research on adoption at the library. I couldn't find too many books on the subject, so I made an appointment with a local care worker the following week. She gave me some very informative advice, describing all the available avenues to adoption and discussing the red tape one must cut through. For some couples, she said, adoption goes smoothly. Others will suffer long, painful, and disappointing waits, sometimes for several years. The chances of the latter, she warned, are more likely. She wasn't trying to discourage me; she obviously just wanted to illustrate the pros and cons of adopting.

I remember her saying, "There are advantages and disadvantages to agency adoptions in comparison to other adoption options. In agency placement, the birth mother or birth parents place the child with the agency, and then the agency will select a couple from their list. You can suggest what your needs are as far as what you want the baby to look like, but the agency makes the match for the suitable parent. Both the adoptive and the birth parents stay anonymous. However, it is my understanding that now some agencies are allowing limited contact with the biological parents."

I was excited to see how many different avenues were available to a woman who wants to adopt.

Her next piece of information was that more than 9,000 children per year were adopted from foreign countries, most of which were from Korea, South America, and India. She went on to say, "This form of adoption, despite the red tape, has a high degree of success. For one thing, the wait is shorter, which pleases most couples who are anxious to be parents."

I knew that for me, international adoption would be a positive way to have a child, but I wasn't so sure about my husband. I left the office with an application for agency placement, along with all kinds of information on other adoption alternatives.

I was nervous on the way home, but somehow quite excited to bring this new concept and good idea home to my husband. Adoption was a concept that we had never considered or thought about. Somehow, I knew in my heart that it would be another disappointment, but I thought it was worth a try anyway. I ran it past him and explained how nice adoption could and would be. After a moment of his silence, I could see that I had been right: the idea didn't appeal to him at all. His eventual and only reply was, "Don't get any ideas! I don't want to adopt a baby."

I became angrier and more discouraged as the weeks and months went by. It just didn't seem fair that all I had ever wanted was a little child to care for and love. It was becoming quite clear that the more I wanted a baby, the more our marriage slipped away. I had once thought that having a little baby in our home would make us a much happier couple, and that it would fill our home with contentment, joy, and happiness—not realizing that there must be an underlying problem. Deep down, I knew that children were not a requirement of a happy marriage. If a marriage has problems, those problems will still be there even after a baby arrives.

After my husband told me that adoption wasn't an option, I felt as though my dream of having children in my life was going to be just that: a dream. His unforgettable words broke my spirit terribly. I knew that adoption wasn't for everyone, but at the same time, I felt that he could at least consider where his wife was coming from. He knew that I loved children more than anything in the world, and yet he said no to adoption without asking me what I wanted or how I felt. It just seemed wrong to me. His words played in my mind over and over, like a broken record, for the many lonely months that followed.

As I'm sitting here today and writing this book, I reflect back on the many trials and tribulations of that part of the journey. I still clearly remember hearing those words: "Don't get any ideas!" These words really were the final answer for me. I knew then that I had no hope whatsoever of having a child as long as I was with my husband. I would ask myself, "Is this why couples get divorced? Is this a form of control? Is my dream of a baby that impossible?"

I also asked myself the question, "Why stay married?" Looking back now and knowing what I know, I would advise any woman with a partner who does not want a child to reconsider where her priorities lie. No relationship is carved in stone, no matter how solid it may seem at the time; I found that out the hard way. Women need to be true to themselves and do what their hearts tell them to do. Likewise, if a man really wants children and his wife does not, each member of the couple should reconsider what is most important to them.

I began to feel resentment toward my husband, because he didn't want to adopt a child. What was I to do? Get a divorce? Forget about adopting a child? Forget about this marriage? Look for a man who wanted kids? Or look for a man who had kids? Where did a woman go from here?

I knew that if I had to let go of this dream of having kids, it was not going to be an easy task. I also knew that I had to stay positive if I wanted to get through this with optimism and hope for the future. I wanted to also be realistic and face anything that unfolded in front of me—even if I had to do it alone, without a husband and without kids.

At the time, it was very important to step back from all the stress and get away for a few months, in order to get our thoughts and lives back on track. It was great to step back from the entire baby ordeal. Travel is something I recommend to partners needing to rekindle their relationship at any time, but especially if they have been going through all the stress and anxiety of infertility. It is overwhelming and causes a lot of couples to separate and divorce.

Stress over our inability to conceive and the fear of maybe being alone someday was finally taking its toll on both of us, so we packed our belongings and left for Palm Springs, California. We liked it so much that we didn't return home for three months. It was also a very educational experience, because I met so many wonderful people. I was able to talk to more childless women than I had ever dreamed of. I got more stories for my book, and as a bonus, I learned more about myself and my dear husband than I had ever expected.

One day, when my husband and I were at the top of the tramway in Palm Springs, I noticed a woman of about forty hobbling along on crutches. I looked down and saw that she had only one leg. She introduced herself as Greta from Germany. Her bright blue eyes and blonde hair pretty much confirmed that she was indeed of German decent.

"How are you enjoying your holiday?" I asked.

"I couldn't be happier," she replied with a wide grin and sparkly eyes. "The weather is beautiful, the people are friendly, and I have so much to see in such a short time."

"How long will you be staying?" I asked, thinking that she had meant her holiday was short.

Her unbelievable answer was, "Oh, I'll be here until I die. You see, I have only six months to live."

I stood there in a state of awe, not knowing whether to give her a hug or my rosary beads. I said, "I'm so sorry to hear that."

"Oh, no, don't be sorry, dear," she said. "I have had a very full, complete, and satisfying life. I've traveled most of the world, and I don't feel I have missed anything. I have a wonderful family and many friends."

"How many kids do you have?" I asked.

She responded, "I don't have any children. I never felt the need to take care of children; my need was always to take care of myself, and I have." Her parting words were, "Enjoy your time here, and always make the most of your life—it's shorter than you think."

I believe we meet people in our lives for a reason, and that there are no coincidences. That woman was meant to deliver a message to me that life was shorter than I thought. I have learned since that day that she was right. She inspired me immensely, and I gained a lot of my strength through not only her words of wisdom, but also the fact that she was childless and limbless.

Chapter 6
Leaving A Legacy Without Children

*Something good always comes out of something
bad if you look hard enough.*

As months went by, I began to feel somewhat useless. I decided to take up some new and different hobbies and crafts. I spent thousands of dollars on a lot of them, because I got so involved with creating the crafts and teaching the art form to others who also wanted to discover their hidden talents. I wondered if all women who were childless got so bored. What did they do to keep busy? What did women fill their lives with, if not with the entertainment of a child?

I found myself creating some very unique pieces of art and teaching my methods to many interested and talented women. I entered craft fairs and spent many years creating new and fun things.

After a few years, I tired of the crafts and seemed to get more enjoyment out of simpler things, such as shopping—sometimes all day long. I asked myself, "Is this what women who don't have children do to stay happy? Or is this all I will have to spend my money on?" I lived up to the maxim "shop until you drop" for a very short time. I loved shopping more than anything, and I felt that somehow, buying and wearing beautiful clothes would make me feel more feminine or complete. I seemed to have this feeling that if I dressed the part of someone else, I would become that someone else and be happier. Perhaps I would somehow feel just as important as women who had children.

My way of justifying the shopping was that I didn't have kids to buy clothing for, so I felt it was quite all right to spend all the money on myself. As good as it felt to shop, I wasn't comfortable knowing that I had a serious problem going on; not only was my shopping costing a fortune, but it had also started to feel just like an addiction. I had this addiction for over five years, and it wasn't until I realized that it was only compensation for my inability to have a child that I actually came to my senses. That epiphany dawned when I ran into a friend of mine named Alice in a quaint little dress boutique.

Alice, who is also childless, said, "Funny meeting you in a ladies' apparel shop again—it's the only place we ever seem to see each other!"

We both laughed, and I commented, "Isn't it crazy how much time and money we spend on shopping?"

"Yeah, and mostly because we don't have kids to worry about—or kids to spend it on. Are we blessed, or are we cursed?" We both learned a very life-changing lesson that day when Alice said, "It's not the clothes that we want so much, or the fashions. It's more than likely just a facade. We must be unconsciously trying to hide behind the clothes to fill the emptiness that we feel, or something ... and somehow, looking good and feeling good makes us feel happier, and it temporarily fills that void of being childless. What do you think?"

I said, "I have to agree with you, Alice—I think you're absolutely right. You have confirmed something that I've felt for a long time. Now we can share this secret with other childless women who want to fill their time doing something creative, inexpensive, and entertaining that will leave them a legacy without children."

We talked and talked about how many friends we had that were noticeably doing the same thing, for the same reasons. We agreed right then and there to get together with a few of these women once a week for meditation and an art project of one kind or another. That way, we could all learn, heal, and support each other. We found that many of these involuntarily childless women displayed various little habits developed strictly out of boredom, so we got back into our arts and crafts and decided that we could take our arts to any level we wanted to.

We seemed to gain all our strength from each other, our families, and sometimes perfect strangers that we would meet at the workplace, on the ski hill, or during a vacation in the middle of nowhere. We would document all the events that had seemed coincidental at the time but were later revealed to be anything but.

One day, Alice and I met a woman by the name of Martina from Morocco in a little coffee shop one day. Martina was an incredible artist who was looking for a place to stay while she sold some of her beautiful oil paintings at a local art fair. Alice made her a makeshift room that Martina stayed in for over two years; we all became good friends as Alice and I learned the art of oil painting from the energy within us. This painting was a form of healing that awakened us to our spiritual selves, serving as great therapy in everyday life. I ended up teaching this form of art once I mastered it. The people we meet are meant to come into our lives, even if we sometimes can't figure out the reason.

I know that had I not been there with Martina, on that part of my journey, I would not be able to be here, today, sharing and helping those who need support. If I can help even one person in any way by sharing my own experiences, my art, or my healing energy, my life really has served its purpose. I will consider all of these people as my gifts.

I firmly believe that art in any form is a great way to find yourself and your true happiness, whether you are writing, drawing, painting, making jewelry, taking photographs, or making things out of nothing. Art is up to the individual, and it can lead you anywhere. Many of my childless friends have found their true purpose in various forms of art.

I believe that art is a beautiful way to express yourself in more ways than one. You can make your income through it, you can discover your hidden talents, and you can leave a legacy without children. If you are an artist and sell your work locally or all over the world, your pieces will form a legacy lasting thousands of years—unlike people, who are only here for a short time!

Chapter 7
Discovering Our Gifts

> *Your vision will become clear only when you look into your heart. Who looks outside, dreams. Who looks inside, awakens.*
> —Carl Jung

***W**ho looks inside, awakens.* Those very words came to me over the radio waves while driving through the Rocky Mountains of British Columbia one winter. At the time, they made no sense whatsoever to me. It wasn't until several years later, while going for a walk with a friend, that those very words came to me again—only this time, they meant a whole lot more to me, because I heard them with different ears. In fact, I may have taken those awesome words to a whole different level because of where I happened to be in my life at the time. I took those words to mean that if we look within ourselves, we will discover our gifts.

After I had gone through my own trials and tribulations, I knew that my gift was the ability to reach people and support them through their crises. What I had thought were my hardships only unmasked the gifts that I had within me. I learned to love, heal, grow spiritually, and expand mentally. Therefore, I had discovered my gifts.

Many of us have heard the expression "Something good always happens from something bad." Well, I am sure that something good came out of my bad experiences. Because I couldn't have kids,

I was able to discover my gifts: knowledge, listening, kindness, energy, compassion, and so on. I'm sure that if I would have had children, I would have been so busy in their lives that I would have forgotten all about myself. Just because we have love for ourselves does not mean that we are conceited or self-centered; it just means we respect and love ourselves as people and as beautiful human beings. It took me a long time to accept and understand that. I was not to have children in this life so I could awaken to my true self and become the person I am today—living in the spirit, helping people, and giving of my gift.

Whenever I hear a childless woman say that she can't find what she is looking for to make her happy, I tell her to write a list of all the things that she wants; write a list of all the things in her life that she has and loves; write a list of all the things that she needs; and write a list of all the things that would make her happy. Many women write down "money" as the first priority, then "love." They are surprised to realize that the word "children" was never written down. These women soon start to seek their passion with a career, travel plans, an education, a renewed religious devotion, or spiritual growth.

When these same women rewrite their lists, they name the things that they really want, and material things are replaced with trust, faith, respect, and love—none of which money can buy. These things, once found, last longer than money, and they give a person more inner peace than money ever could. Once again, these women will find it odd that they never wrote down the word "children." Try writing down your wants and see what you come up with.

Many women discover their gifts when they least expect it. We all are born with gifts; it's just that some of us don't realize we have them until an unfortunate circumstance reveals them. Sooner or later, our gifts unfold right in front of our eyes.

I always feel that my gifts are my family, my friends, and my health.

Chapter 8
Support Groups

I loved being a part of my own women's support circle every week; I enjoyed being able to listen and share what knowledge I had. My words of wisdom were made into a big poster that was mounted in the front of the room, up on the wall, for everyone to read as they sat down and made themselves comfortable. These words were different every day; they came in messages spoken by my inner voice—the voice that I not only believed, but trusted. Some of those words were "Never look back," "Believe in yourself," and "Learn to forgive and love yourself."

It was amazing to see how many women who were childless by chance wanted to get together for support and guidance. We all realized that it didn't matter whether we were recognized by the government or whether we had an official name; all we knew was that we were there for one another. We weren't judgmental; we shared our stories; we offered help if we had experience with the problem at hand; we advised going to a family counselor if needed. We found that we were no different from women who poured their stories out at a quilting bee, a sewing bee, a church meeting, or a hair appointment. It was all a form of therapy. We had the best of both worlds: we not only made new friends, but we felt a sense of healing and discovery when it came to our personal needs.

I suggest that any involuntarily childless woman who needs support or reassurance join a support group—or start one up on her own. There is nothing wrong with friends and relatives getting together to support one another through a crisis or circumstance.

In joining a support group, you will find contentment and inner peace like you've never felt before. Just knowing that you're not alone with your feelings, no matter what they are, will comfort you. At the same time, your participation in the group will give you a sense of being needed. Joining a support group is the greatest thing you can do for yourself, whether you join a national one (such as Response in the United States) or a support group in your local community. Even if you simply start meeting with friends on your own, it's truly the greatest gift you can give yourself.

When evaluating a support group you are joining or one you are a part of, you might want to ask these simple questions.

- Does this group keep everything confidential?
- Do I feel enlightened and inspired?
- Do I feel as though I am healing in any way?
- Do I feel trusted and respected?
- Does being a part of this group make me feel more positive?
- Does each person get to express her feelings and be heard?
- Does having this group in my life make me feel accepted?
- Do I receive what I am looking for?
- Does this group welcome new members like it were family?
- Does this group make everyone feel equal?

If you have to hesitate in response to these questions or answer no to most of them, reconsider your membership in the group. You may want to find another one or create one of your own. Given the fact that so many support groups are in existence now, one likely already exists that is suited to your needs. The best support groups I have found are not necessarily the most well-known, but rather ones that are home based and are spiritually influenced. Support groups seem to exist in every size and for every situation and circumstance. Regardless of which group you choose, there is no better medicine or source of education than shared life experiences.

Chapter 9
Finding Happiness In Choices

I always find the stories from women I meet more interesting than a good movie. These stories seem to resonate in my heart to the point where I find myself teary-eyed and speechless.

One such instance occurred when I was standing in line for eight hours outside the *Price Is Right* studio in California, waiting to be interviewed to be a contestant on the show. I happened to be in line beside a lovely woman who was just hilarious; she had a sense of humor that had everyone laughing. We thought for sure she would make it onto the stage because of her excitable personality, along with her eye-catching red outfit that seemed to pop out among the crowd of anxious people.

I asked her, "What is your secret to being so happy?"

She answered, "Because I look at life as if I am living my last day."

"Well," I said, "That is a good way to look at it. I never looked at it quite like that before." I thought that now would be a good opportunity to ask her whether she had kids. So I popped the question, and I will never forget her reply.

She said, "What do kids have to do with being happy?"

I kind of cringed at her answer, because I didn't know what to say next; she had caught me off guard. I stood quietly for a moment, and before I could say anything, she asked me the same question: "Do you have kids?"

My answer to her was, "No, I don't have kids."

She responded with three words: "Count your blessings."

We didn't get to go on stage with Bob Barker, but we enjoyed being in the audience. I often think back to her comments and the happy outlook on life that she maintained even without children. Her memorable words still ring in my ears: "What do kids have to do with being happy?"

On another occasion, I met a woman named Tina on a recent train trip across Canada. Tina, who appeared to be in her late thirties, was taking pictures of everything from old, broken-down cow barns to grain elevators in the wheat fields. I asked her, point blank, "Are you a photographer?"

She said, "Funny you should ask. I am in photography school, and I want to be a photographer—thanks for asking." She then added, "I had to make the decision to either further my career or find a man and start a family. I decided to start a career instead."

"Why is that?" I asked her.

She said, "Well, for one thing, I know the career won't let me down."

I didn't ask her any more questions, but wrote of the experience in my journal under "Women's choices."

I have met several women over the years who admit that they only feel needed or fulfilled when they have someone to nurture and care for. This was the case with Shelby, a classmate of mine in medical office school. Shelby, a single thirty-five-year-old, always talked about her babies and how she had to go straight home, because she didn't like leaving them too long.

One night, out of the blue, I asked, "How old are your kids?"

She answered, "Ten and twelve. They are my whole life, and the best thing that ever happened to me."

"Do you have a picture of your kids?"

"Of course," she said, digging into her wallet to get the pictures out. At this point, a few of us curious students stood beside her, wanting to see her babies. She surprised and shocked a few of us when she flipped them out in a nice little folder, saying, "These are my precious babies—aren't they just the most adorable little things you ever did see?"

"Ah, well, yes," I said. "Only all this time, we thought your precious little babies were real little babies."

"Oh, no, never. I have two dogs, and that's enough. I can't handle any more than these two—they take up my time, devotion, and money the same way that children would. Anyone wanting to feel needed, happy, content, and safe should get themselves a pet—especially a dog!"

When I was right in the midst of my infertility issues, trying to fit all the pieces of the puzzle together, I struggled with many questions. Should I forget about having children, or should I forget about being with a partner who didn't want to adopt a baby?

At this time, I met a girl by the name of Carolynn at a curling game we happened to be watching. Her husband was playing against mine, but we enjoyed our conversation more than the game they were playing.

Carolynn asked, "How many kids do you guys have?"

I answered, "We don't have any kids."

"Oh, I'm sorry for asking—I had no business asking."

"Oh, don't be silly—everyone asks the same question," I reassured her. "I love kids, but I couldn't have them for medical reasons."

What she said next was something I always remember: "Oh, for heaven's sake, I finally have found someone who understands where I'm coming from. Most people just don't understand, do they? I knew there was a reason I came to watch this game. Why do people treat us as though we have a disease or something? Why can't they just treat us like normal women, without acting as though we are selfish or as though we don't like kids? I hate it when I don't get asked to functions where there are babies, because

I love kids—but I seem to get left out of birthdays and children's events just because I don't have a kid."

We never did see much of the game that night, because our minds and hearts were elsewhere. We kept in touch for over twenty years after that night on; several years after I met her, Carolynn divorced her husband and married someone who had twin girls. She said she had to decide whether to merely exist or to make a life for herself that included the contentment and happiness she got from being a mom.

One of my clients, while having her hair cut one day, gave many of us food for thought when she said, "My son just got busted for possession of drugs." She was in tears as she said, "I wish that I had never had kids, because they have brought me nothing but heartache." The beauty shop fell into complete silence as we all listened in horror to her story. She said repeatedly, "I wish I had never had kids. I wish this were a dream I could wake up from." I brought her a cup of coffee to calm her down; she was shaking and talking as though she were trying to get a message out to the young girls in the salon who were dreaming of having kids.

The next day, this client phoned to apologize. The girl answering the phone said, "Oh, Mrs. Clark, please don't apologize. You completely confirmed my worst nightmares and my doubts. Because of you, I went home and told my husband that I have made up my mind that I don't want kids." This particular receptionist, Angela, never did have kids. The last we heard, she was happy and healthy as an airline flight attendant who traveled the world, and she said she owed it all to Mrs. Clark. This story proves that choices are made sometimes by a stroke of luck and by circumstances. This was a case of a little of both.

Do you ever wonder why sometimes we're led to a certain place or we meet a certain person at just the right time? We often feel there must be a reason for it. Well, this very often happens to me, and it always proves to be for a very good reason—sometimes even a miraculous reason.

One such incident occurred when I ran into an old friend of mine from high school sitting in a hot tub at a resort hotel and spa in San Miguel, California. Our first comment was "What a small world!"

I knew there must be a reason for our encounter, so we chatted and caught up on news of all our mutual friends. Then she said, "How do you manage to get away down here in the middle of winter?"

I said, "Well, we don't have kids to worry about, so we can afford it."

She laughed and said, "Isn't that the truth!" I then realized that she was also child-free and was enjoying the good life. She said, "I'm finally happy in my life now without children, but it was a long road. I've had to lose two husbands and a sister over it." She went on to say, "I had to learn some big lessons and realize that I was obsessed with kids because I wasn't happy within myself. I didn't love who I was, and I had no faith in anything. I was fearful of what would happen to me if I didn't have a child. After years of searching and looking in all the wrong places for answers, I woke up and found myself."

I remember staring into the clear, blue sky that night, gazing at the stars, thinking and saying her words out loud: "I wasn't happy within myself. I wasn't happy within myself." Unfortunately, I left early in the morning and never got to see her again. I knew for sure that our meeting had happened for a reason. It didn't matter if I saw her again; what mattered was that I already had.

This letter was left for me by a client who knew I was writing a book on childless women and wanted me to deliver her message somewhere in the manuscript. Thank you, Laura, for your very interesting concept and for loving all those little children the way you do. The world is a better place with women like you who devote all their time, love, and support to foster children.

Had I known then what I know today, I would have made some serious choices a whole lot sooner. I would have married younger and had a couple kids, but I got married late and went through menopause, so was unable to give birth. My husband and I made the choice to raise foster children, and have raised over twenty-five beautiful foster children in fifteen years. I suggest it to anyone that wants the enjoyment and happiness of raising children. It is fun, heartwarming, time consuming, rewarding, satisfying and brings you lots of happiness. It was and still is the best choice we ever made in our life.

Thanks, Laura. I'm sure your advice will resonate in the hearts of many women who are considering fostering a child.

❧ ☙

I loved an e-mail that I received not long ago from a girl named Linda, whom I briefly met at a Christmas party, and who was very enthused about speaking out to other women about having children.

When I was in my thirties, wild, free and more or less living like a happy little hippie, I was so sure that I never ever wanted to have a kid, so made that choice not to have children. I learned that life can be whatever you want to make it, and I have found through it all, that I am more spiritual, much more independent and my life has evolved as a person far beyond my wildest dreams. I now think that the choice I made wasn't such a bad one after all. I'm usually ran off my feet with a busy career, my friends, volunteering, traveling, painting and gardening, and last but not least my two golden labs who are my life and joy, who act and think they are my children.

Another woman's personal story shed some light at one of our little get-togethers several years ago. I keep this story close to my heart, and I'm sure some of you readers can relate to it.

When I was growing up, I had nine brothers and sisters to help raise, as my mom was handicapped and my dad away working. I had to be looking out for them as well as making sure my siblings were dressed properly, taken to school on time, and helped with everything from house work to homework. Being as I was the oldest, they all seemed to want to be my roommate, I was so tired of kids by the time I was twenty-five, that I made the choice not to have kids. However once I reached my forties, and all the siblings were happily married, I began to feel somewhat lonely, and wished I had of had a child of my own. However, I don't look back with regret; I look back with happy memories and joy. I now have twenty two nieces and nephews that I spoil rotten, and am the favorite auntie to most. I love the connection and the love I have developed with them and from them, and have found happiness in so many more ways than just having children of my own.

Chapter 10
The Trip Of A Lifetime

I had the golden opportunity a few years ago to go to Palm Springs again for a winter vacation. I was familiar with all the favorite spots for shopping and dining, and I always felt safe in Palm Springs, so I had no fear of being there alone. This time, I had the distinct feeling that something magical was going to take place and that I needed to go for more reasons than just the sight of palm trees, the opportunity to bask in the sun, and the chance to do some shopping. I made all the arrangements and was packed and ready to go within two days.

The flight was great, because I got to sit beside an interesting woman who was also child-free. She said she loved being without children and wouldn't change her life for anyone. She listed some great places to check out while I was in Palm Springs and gave me the name of a beautiful resort to stay at. This hotel was easy to find on the strip—and one I had always wanted to check out.

Within only a few hours of arriving and settling into this beautiful suite at the resort, I couldn't help but notice a lovely, elderly woman who was talking to someone outside my door. This heavyset woman was tanned like a Hawaiian, and she kept her white, curly hair in a granny bun on top of her head. She was staying in the suite next door and seemed to talk to everyone as though they were old friends. It wasn't long before she introduced herself to me as Hilda. We instantly felt a bond when we exchanged in conversation our places of birth, because she was also Canadian and lived in British Columbia.

Hilda was an Austrian immigrant, a doctor of naturopathic medicine, and a master of Reiki. Her amazing philosophy, wisdom, charm, and zest for life at the ripe old age of seventy-two were in and of themselves amazing. She proclaimed her status as a childless woman with no regrets, and she constantly proved to me that not all childless women sat around and felt sorry for themselves, as I once had done. Hilda was very well-traveled and had been coming to Palm Springs for the winter for over twenty years. She was a spiritual individual who looked and acted more like a fifty-year-old than a seventy-two-year-old. She was simply amazing, and everyone who met her felt drawn to her, like a magnet.

I wanted to know Hilda's secrets to happiness, good health, energy, and enthusiasm. I needed more of all of those assets in my own life, and I felt that if anyone could show me those traits; it would most definitely be her. After two weeks, we were inseparable. I felt as if every day were a new learning experience. She taught me her many secrets for not only physical good health, but for spiritual good health as well.

Every day felt like a private energy-healing session. Hilda talked candidly over dinner one night about how many people who seemingly had everything should be happy, but were not. These people had a dream home, financial security, health, a good spouse, children, a nice car, and even power, but they were still not happy.

I thought about this part: having children and still not being happy. I thought long and hard, as though the underlying principle were going to be something I lived by. I asked myself, "Why are people who do have children still not always content or fulfilled? Why are they sometimes still not happy?" This question haunted me. I started to think about my own situation. I had been so grief-stricken at one time, just because I couldn't have children—and yet even the people who did have them sometimes were still not fulfilled. If there were a logical answer to this paradox, I was determined to find out what it was. I thought that it would certainly help me feel somewhat more satisfied to think that I could have had a child, and then not been as happy as I expected.

I turned this idea over in my head constantly until it finally made sense. It wasn't my lack of children that sometimes made me feel empty or incomplete. It was simply the fact that I wanted my life to have more meaning—some purpose. I wanted to know that I had made a difference in this world, rather than only passing through it.

By the time my two-month holiday was over, I had a far greater understanding of my purpose in life. In fact, I realized that my whole trip must have been part of my destiny—like a map of my destination before I ever arrived there. It was no accident that I had met the woman on the plane—or Hilda. Hilda was meant to give me the life-changing secrets that could be found in her daily inspirations and spiritual wisdom; I was meant to receive them as I did, with much grace and loyalty. I believe that Hilda was an inspirational angel—truly heaven-sent.

I now know that those two months of vacationing, basking in the sun, awakening to my higher self, enjoying the markets, and cherishing the friends that I made represented the turning point in my life. That holiday changed my life forever.

The trip itself was one I will never, ever forget. It was such a learning experience; it changed my thinking and my way of life forever. It also taught me many things about myself; one of them was that I had to learn to love myself, as well as others, in order to have complete balance. I had never ever been able to do this in the past—because, I suppose, we were always taught that people who loved themselves were conceited or self-centered. We were always taught to love others. I also learned that we all have gifts; these gifts are not anything you can buy. They are the gifts with no price tag. They are the gifts of forgiving, giving, loving, listening, having courage, and healing. These gifts are not material things, money, or fame. They are our friends, our families, our good health, our spirituality, our compassion, our love for people, our eyes, our ears, our spirits, and our souls. These things were given to us at birth, and they are all we need in this life to have happiness. I thank God for them every day, and I don't take any of them for granted anymore.

Chapter 11
Making A Difference Without Children

I came home from that trip feeling as if I had been a part of a spiritual journey that left me with the most optimistic understanding of my life as a childless woman. I learned the difference between letting go of the past and letting go of negatives in the present. I learned how to let go of things that had never been mine in the first place—and would not have made me any happier even if they had been.

The dark cloud that had been hovering all around me for so long had been miraculously lifted from my shoulders. I thanked God for that; I could finally see the light at the end of the tunnel, and I felt a sense of well-being, strength, and hope for the future that I hadn't felt in years. I wanted to share this incredible feeling of wholeness and happiness with every woman in the world, especially if they were experiencing the stigma of being childless, as I had. I felt as if my life finally had a purpose other than being a mom, and that I would make a difference in the world without children.

I no longer felt that the label "childless" was a threat to me. I knew I wanted to somehow reach out to every woman in the world who was childless, either by choice or by chance, who was feeling anything but beautiful, whole, and happy. I wanted to help those women realize that they were beautiful, whole, and complete without children—and that once they unmasked all the gifts they were born with, they could move forward with empowerment, inner peace, health, and happiness.

For me, I suppose, the biggest lesson was the realization that kids were not everything, as I had always thought they were, and that I could make a difference without children. As much as I had envisioned children to be what makes a woman happy, I had to face the cold, hard fact that they really were not! I needed to be told this truth in a way that was not cruel or sarcastic; it was just a message given to me by way of a stranger, someone I had only just met, and someone whose philosophy and words of wisdom were ready to be heard and believed. I truly felt that this message was really from the divine. I embraced those words as if I had been hit by lightning; those words would change my life.

I continued working as a stylist, but more and more, I was guided to my intuitive gift and abilities. I mostly enjoyed working one-on-one with childless women, because I myself had been so passionate about children for so many years. If women were feeling depressed and lonely and having a difficult time coping with being childless, I would give them all the knowledge and expertise I had gained from my own experiences and from other women who had shared their stories.

My little support group, which consisted of only a handful of women, still gathered faithfully at my home on a weekly basis. We listened, talked, compared, shared, prayed, meditated, and supported. It did my heart good to see these women, who had had the same insecurities as I had when they first joined the group, flourish with pride and inspiration after only a few months in our circle. They didn't take long to replace those feelings of loneliness and fear with joy, confidence, hope, and fulfillment. They felt as though they had an important place in the world—not only as fulfilled childless women, but as women who made a difference in the world because of who they became without children.

At that particular time in my life, I still found myself spending a lot of my free time with children of any age, and it was great, because their presence no longer bothered me as it once had. There was a time when I felt an ache in my heart whenever I babysat children, because they weren't mine. However, now it was so different; I could ask for children to come for a visit for the day without feeling empty when they left. Whether these children were nieces, nephews, or neighbor kids, I could take in as many as ten kids at a time and love every minute of it, without wishing I could have been a mom. Spending time with these children also made me appreciate exactly what goes on behind the closed doors of a full-time mom. The ups and downs of taking care of kids in general on a daily basis, from high-pitched laughter to spilled milk and dirty diapers, showed me that nothing in life was perfect, even motherhood. Now, whenever I watch a woman play with her children in the park, I no longer feel a little jealous tug at my heart the way I once did. Rather, I watch with a careful eye instead of a tearful eye as her children pull at her apron strings.

When you realize your gifts through your own experiences and use those gifts, you feel more connected to the spiritual side of yourself, and you automatically become more fulfilled and happy. At the same time, you become more aware of why you are without children. Whenever I met women who were sad or regretful about not having their own children, but who were still within their child-bearing years, I would give them a list of different options, including sperm donation, artificial insemination, surrogacy, and fertility drugs. I would even include alternative methods, such as the ones I tried, as well as the adoption and fostering possibilities that are always out there. Working from my own experience, I encourage these women to refuse to let anyone take their motherhood dream away, as I had. If a woman wants children and believes she will never be happy until she has them, she should do what she can to make that dream a reality.

On the other hand, whenever I talk to women who are in their midthirties and don't want to ever have kids because they are not crazy about kids and don't really want the responsibility, I can't help but point out all the many other important things that life has to offer them. There are so many ways to feel needed, wanted, loved, special, whole, complete, and appreciated without children.

I seem to express more and more the importance of prayer in our lives. Meditation, visualization, forgiving, and listening to our inner voices are all important as well. We all have an inner voice, and sometimes we ignore it, or we don't hear it. But once we do listen to our inner voices and learn to trust and believe in those voices, we can live much more harmoniously, because we will be doing what we are meant to be doing.

My intuitive counseling, mentoring, and spiritual healing abilities all became apparent very soon after my awakening to my own true self in the late eighties. I was embraced by the gift of intuition, and I knew that my life had changed dramatically for a reason.

One thing you will learn from spending time with children is the importance of feeling needed and being loved. I was overjoyed with happiness when I learned that having a child of my own really wasn't the most important thing in the world; before, when anyone tried to tell me this, I took offense and felt criticized. Now, however, I say those very words to myself on a daily basis, because I feel they are true and make good sense. I found out that being happy with myself and believing in who I am as a woman are far more important than being a mom.

Our Creator made us with all the resources we will ever need. We sometimes just need to be reminded of this, especially when we find ourselves floundering, disillusioned, and discouraged in our daily lives, the way I had felt when I learned that I could never be a biological mom. I had thought for sure that there was nothing else to live for, nothing else that could ever replace the love of kids or make me happy.

Sometimes, it takes an unfortunate circumstance to wake us up and make us realize how much we do have and what our purpose in life really is. Had I not had my wake-up call, I would likely still be wallowing in self-pity and leaning on all the crutches that I fell victim to. I would more than likely still be suffering many physical and psychological problems had it not been for my desire to find myself and attain inner peace. I also wanted to find my purpose in life and trust the inner voice that kept telling me that I was childless for a reason.

I can't say I don't sometimes wonder what it would have been like to have had a child of my own; this is only natural, I'm sure. But once I discovered the real meaning of my life and moved on, I realized that as much as I love children and enjoy spending time with them, I no longer feel that my whole life has to completely revolve around them in order for me to feel whole or complete as a woman. I hope you have the same experience. If so, the word "childless" will no longer feel like a threat or a badge; nor will it be a word to feel embarrassed or ashamed about, like some kind of disease. You will feel that it is merely just a word in the dictionary that describes a woman who has no children.

Chapter 12
Filling The Void

I recommend that any woman who feels alienated, depressed, or purposeless get involved with children of any age, whether they are nieces, nephews, or children of her friends. Spending time with children is by far one of the best pastimes in the world. You can put an ad in your local newspaper as a nanny or babysitter. If you have a daytime job, you can work with children on weekends. You can arrange outings and plan with working mothers to get involved with their kids' hockey games or dance recitals. You can offer to volunteer as the crossing guard or chaperone at the school grounds, as a clown at a birthday party, or as a visitor to a child who is sick in a local hospital. This volunteerism is all part of being and feeling needed, even if you aren't a biological mother.

You will find an inner peace and happiness and feel healthier by not only filling the void that gnaws away at your soul, but by finding yourself loved by more kids than you ever imagined. You can act as a special pretend auntie to more kids than most women will ever have in their lifetimes.

In return, you will also feel energized and will look and feel much younger than you are. Children will get you to do things that you never dreamed of doing when you were a kid yourself. You will begin to act younger and think like a teenager. All the excitement and laughter will prompt you to forget all your worries and live a happier and healthier lifestyle. You will get out more and have more energy and enthusiasm than you ever dreamed of. All you need on your list when taking kids on an outing is lots of water, good running shoes, a cell phone, and a few dollars to get them a little treat at the end of the day. You will appreciate the break, and they will love feeling spoiled and special. You will laugh more than you have in years, which is the best medicine in the world anyway; they will thrive on all the love and undivided attention, and so will you.

The rewards to having so many kids involved in your life are endless. You will never have a dull moment, because children will keep you very fit, especially when they want you to blow up their balloons. They will invite you to every birthday party, dance recital, and school concert they are ever in, and when they grow up, they will invite you to their school graduations and their weddings. Before too long, you'll get to babysit all over again—only now it's for their babies. If you're lucky, you can remember some of the stories you made up when you told those bedtime stories so many years before. These are just a few of the many rewards that you can enjoy from being a part of a child's life without being their biological mom.

It is always a nice surprise when you get an envelope in the mail from someone whose name looks familiar—and upon opening it, find a letter from one of those kids you once babysat. They are now married with their own children, and they just want to say hello and ask for the recipe for the Mickey Mouse pancakes you spent time making for them when they weren't feeling well. They will reminisce about all the fun things they did while you were watching them, and ask why you didn't get mad when you caught them playing with fifteen frogs in your bathtub. They will talk about how you made an impression on their lives, when the whole time you were all just feeling happy and having fun, not realizing that lifetime memories were in the making.

I always had a good supply of toys around for the kids that I dreamed of having, but after years had passed and I had accepted that I was never going to be a mom, I donated most of my two hundred teddy bears to the fire department, so they could be wrapped and taken to the burn unit at the children's hospital at Christmastime. I used all the other little toys for accents on wrapping paper when I had to bring a gift to a baby shower or a little child's birthday party. I always keep a few little treasures on hand to give out to children who quite often seem to cross my path. I still love them as much as ever.

When a girl in her thirties came up to me and said that when she was six years old and I was her neighbor, I had made an impression on her because I gave her a handful of polished rocks that she still treasures to this day, I realized that such little things in life are more important than anything money can buy. I learned that from this particular girl, who thought she had learned it from me many years before. She taught me just another one of life's lessons.

Chapter 13
Finding Our Purpose

Let no one feel unimportant, for they too have a story.
—Unknown

I believe that right now, more than ever before, is the right time for childless women who are suffering under a stigma for any reason to make a difference in the world just by speaking out about their true, honest feelings. Sharing these feelings with other women who are also going through their own personal journey is healing in itself. We as childless women have to get the word out there, no matter who we are: movie stars, well-known people, entrepreneurs, or the women down the street—it doesn't matter.

What does matter is that women from all walks of life, whether they are with children or without them, need to have a purpose in life. The women who do not have children and who have always wanted them need to realize that they certainly do not have to give birth to children in order to have true meaning, inner peace, happiness, contentment, and purpose in their lives. I know many childless women who say that they have found their happiness, love, and true purpose—not by having children, but by finding out who they are as women.

Just look at some of the women who have made a difference in the world without having children. One who comes to my mind, and probably yours, is Oprah Winfrey. As a talk-show host and philanthropist, she has changed the world in miraculous ways, and I can't imagine this world without such a powerful, genuine, spiritual, and loving individual. She has helped tens of thousands of people from all walks of life, both rich and poor, fortunate and not so fortunate. Her schools, book clubs, television shows, donations, and gifts have changed thousands of people's lives; I wouldn't have enough pages in my book to mention even a fraction of them. My point is that Oprah didn't need to have children of her own in order to be whole, complete, happy, or successful. She has meaning and purpose in her life. She obviously recognized that her purpose was already within her, and she embraced it with love and commitment. Her gifts are many, but her gift of giving and of being an honest true person who believes in not only herself, but in every person in the world, is what makes her stand out in the crowd. To me, Oprah is an angel sent to all of us from heaven.

Another wonderful childless woman who comes to mind, of course, is Mother Teresa. She definitely made a mark on the world, and we certainly know what her purpose was in this life, as well as her legacy. She believed in not only peace, health, and happiness for the world, but she also had the gift of giving, and she used her sacred gift to give back to the world. She believed in every human being; she had a vision and found her purpose in life, which was to bring peace to the world. She gave of herself to make the world a better place to live.

Those of us who are not destined to have children in this life must look at the bright side and be advocates for those who cross our path with the same fate. We can enjoy and appreciate all the glamour we have because we aren't straddled down with a child tugging at our apron strings and wanting our attention twenty-four hours a day. We can go out and share our many gifts with the world. We can do something positive with our freedom to make a difference. We can donate more money to children's hospitals, women's shelters, or animal shelters. We can spend more time getting to know who we are, so we can help others in their journey to health and happiness. We have more time for prayer; we can thank God every day for all the things in our lives that we do have. We have more time and commitment to offer support groups. The rewards of happiness and joy we receive after sharing our gifts are miraculous. By being there for others with an open heart, you will feel needed more than ever before, loved by more people than you ever imagined, and confident of your true purpose in life.

Naturally, it is easier to keep an open mind and heart when everything in our lives is going great and runs smoothly. However, when unexpected turns in the road arise, such as discovering that you have cancer or that your relationship is over, you may find yourself ready to shut down completely. In my own tragedies, I knew that if I shut down the open mind that I had always seemed able to hang onto, I would have undoubtedly forgotten and lost all that I had learned along the way, and I didn't want to risk that. By keeping my open mind and wanting to heal my broken spirit, I learned to love myself for who I was, rather than who I thought I wasn't, and find my purpose instead. I was able to accept what the Creator had given me, rather than what He hadn't given me. Had I not done this when I did, I'm sure that I would not have been able to allow the possibilities of miracles, love, and happiness back into my life.

Chapter 14
Finding Strength

For me, finding strength was my biggest challenge, because strength existed at the core of the whole experience of infertility. I knew that I had to embrace, overcome, and accept my childlessness, even though I didn't like it. I knew that in order to move forward, I had to accept this fate before it destroyed me, both physically and mentally.

I can't stress more to women how important it is to strive for this strength. It doesn't matter if you seek that strength with your dearest friends, your family, your support group, your congregation members, or your counselor, as long as you triumph.

Infertility is a sad thing, yes.
Infertility has devastated your life, yes.
Infertility is unfair, yes.
Infertility is life-changing, yes.

But just remember that it doesn't kill you, it doesn't change your looks, and it won't destroy your life unless you allow it to.

Infertility can and will sometimes bring out the worst in a person, but very often, it will bring out the very best in you.

More often than not, it awakens you to who you really are, and you find an inner peace within yourself that you otherwise would never have found.

I have found that staying focused, staying positive, and believing in yourself are three of the main keys to staying happy when you are faced with childlessness through no fault of your own.

Make your own happiness simply by knowing that anything you want to attain in this life can be yours if you want it badly enough.

If you want children and can't have your own, you can adopt a child.

If you want a career in a certain field, go back to school and get your education.

If you want to be more musical, take some lessons.

If you want to be healthier and more fit, get out walking and talk to a dietitian about your diet.

It doesn't matter what our dreams are; we can find happiness if we strive for it.

These tips reflect just a few of the actions I took to change my life in order to find the happiness I was searching for; I can only advise anyone who knows what she is capable of.

Chapter 15
Words Of Wisdom

Whenever I hear women who are childless expressing that they are having a hard time dealing with a fear of the future, anger, denial, frustration, alienation, inadequacy, insecurity, a sense of incompletion, or depression, I share these fifteen miraculous secrets for inner peace and happiness that have worked in my life. I would like to pass them on to you in the hopes that they become a part of your life.

1. Never look back, unless it's with happy memories.
2. Avoid negative thinking and negative people.
3. Thank God every day for your many gifts
4. Know that you will never need more than what God has given you.
5. Listen to your inner voice, and trust it.
6. Learn to love yourself.
7. Learn to heal and forgive yourself.
8. Make the most of what you have.
9. If your dream dies, dream another one.
10. Open your eyes today in order to see the beauty tomorrow.

11. Never let fear hold you back.
12. Learn to love unconditionally.
13. Learn to forgive and forget.
14. Give away kindness, and mean it.
15. Learn to pray on a daily basis.

Chapter 16
The Voices We Hear

*Try to get something positive out of something
you only thought was negative.*

For over two decades, I've been talking to women about their lives without children. So often, they recount the sad stories they hear from women who do have children—who, for some reason, try to make the childless woman feel better by telling them how children have made their lives so miserable, and how they would give anything to trade places with those women who don't have kids. All of these statements are very personal and overwhelming, but nevertheless, they were said in an attempt to make the childless women feel somewhat thankful for not having children. But it's never made any of the childless women I know feel any better. If anything, such complaints make the childless women more defensive. I learned many years ago not to let any of these statements get to me, no matter how rude they sounded at the time.

I thought I would share some of these statements. If you are a childless woman, you may or may not have had the exact same things said to you at one time or another. If you haven't yet, give it time, because you more than likely will.

An elderly man in a rest home once said to me while I was visiting my father-in-law, "My two daughters will go see their friends who live on the same street as me, and they pass by and never come to visit. I have done more for them than anyone in the world. You wouldn't believe how much that hurts a parent."

A lady once said to me while waiting for a bus, "You must have saved a lot of money, since you didn't have the expense of raising kids. Mine have kept me in the poorhouse! I wish I had all the hundreds of thousands of dollars I have spent on my kids. I know one thing: I sure wouldn't be taking a bus."

One of my clients said, "Be thankful you won't ever know what it's like to have the heartaches that kids bring home. If I had it to do all over again, I would never have a kid in a million years. If you ever get the urge to have kids, I'll rent you mine for a few days, and you will come to your senses in one hell of a hurry."

This comment is also very common, as I hear it from all my friends who have children: "With all the violence and crime in the world today, be thankful you aren't bringing up a child in this wicked world. Maybe you are blessed, and you don't even realize it. Maybe God knew exactly what he was doing when he didn't bless you with a child in this life; maybe you should be thanking Him every day for being childless.

We often hear a person say, "Our kids have kept us in the poorhouse." Well, although that may be true for some people, childless women who long to have children really don't think about what a child would cost, because money never enters the equation. What you do hear them say, though, is, "I want to have children, no matter what the cost."

Whenever someone tries to make me feel better by saying something negative about their children or children in general, I always tell them to be thankful for their lives, because many women would give a million dollars to have a child. These women will then say that they took it for granted, that they got pregnant exactly when they planned to and had a lovely, healthy child. They realize motherhood didn't happen that way for everyone until someone they knew had to adopt a child.

The most common phrase I hear is, "Count your blessings." I do pray every day and do count all my blessings; however, the admonishment to do so has never been one of them! Another phrase I hear a lot is, "You're so lucky." The women who are childless by chance don't consider themselves lucky by any stretch of the word. A lot of childless women who have moved on with their lives can certainly find many wonderful things to thank God for; however, I don't know too many women who thank God that they are childless.

One statement I heard not long ago was, "The words 'Mother Nature' don't mean you have to be a mother." I don't know who thinks up these phrases, but some of them can be cruel or hurtful to the person hearing them.

I was in the audience of the show of Sylvia Browne, a very well-known psychic, last month. One of the comments that Sylvia made to the audience was, "All of us women who have children hate all you women who don't." This was right out of the blue; maybe she picked up that I was writing this book on childless women. I just thought it was unreal that the comment would come out in front of five hundred people from such a well-known psychic.

Chapter 17
Enjoy The Good Life

We only go through life once; it's not a dress rehearsal. Enjoy the journey.

Most of the women I know who don't have children say they are the lucky ones who made the choice in the late eighties to be child-free. When asked whether they would change anything in their lives if they could, they always say, "No, not a thing." They are still working and are looking forward to retirement at an earlier age, so they can enjoy the good life. They can travel more, experience more freedom from work, enjoy better health, and make more money than they would have if they had kids. They have their homes paid for, and they want to spend their retirement years traveling while they are still young and healthy enough to enjoy their lives and do all the things they always wanted to do.

These women, who made the choice not to become biological mothers, seem to be so grounded. They have found peace and contentment in their lives. They are totally happy with their decision. They are content, they are healthy, and they enjoy meaningful lives. They feel as whole and complete as any woman who has children.

I happened to meet one of these women on the golf course one day. She was talking about how she and her husband had never had children by choice, and how they had a winter home in Florida, a ski chalet in Colorado, and a home in Arizona. She commented that because she and her husband hadn't had to raise kids, they were able to help children in Third World countries by sending money every month for their education and medical needs.

I asked her if she was ever sorry that she had made the choice to be child-free. Her answer was simply, "To tell you the truth, we've always been so busy, content, and happy together as a husband-and-wife team that we didn't think it would change our lives any." She added, "Being child-free has allowed us to travel the world and share our wealth with children who are not so fortunate."

One of my old neighbors from years ago, who was in her late seventies at the time and had never had children, was envied by most women, even at her ripe, old age. She said she had always worked for a living, was divorced, and had no children because of medical reasons. She said that when she first found out that she could never have her own kids, she decided to be a gypsy and travel solo as soon as she turned forty years old. She was the most interesting woman for her age. She was very intelligent, independent, bright, happy, healthy, and tremendously inspiring. She obviously loved her life and was not about to settle down for anyone or anything. She took trains, planes, and buses; she hiked and biked in places we had never heard of. She said she loved being alone and had made hundreds of friends on all her travels; she recommended it for anyone at any age, especially if they didn't have children.

Her philosophy was, "You are only young once, so you may as well enjoy the good life while you are healthy and feel you want to do it." Someone asked her once if she ever regretted not having children, and her response was that if she would have had kids, she wouldn't have been able to travel the world and be the gypsy that she was. Knowing her, if she would have had a child, it would have been strapped into a harness on her back, and she would have continued hiking up the mountains, baby and all.

Many of the women I know who once felt the stigma of being childless, harbored fears of being alone in old age, and felt incomplete as women now feel happier than ever before, years later. They have more confidence now, and they have found a comfort zone in their lives with their partners and their pets, and they love who they have become because of being child-free.

As we get older, we realize that the things we once wanted are much less important to us than when we were in our twenties and thirties. Once a woman gets over the fear of being alone when she gets old and realizes that children are no guarantee against loneliness in old age, it is easier to explore other avenues for fulfillment, such as a career, recreation, travel, pets, sports, hobbies, crafts, and hundreds of other hidden talents you may discover when you have the time. I had a client who said she never worried about not having kids, because she was too busy working, dancing, singing, writing music, traveling, and writing books. She often said, "It's not only because it helps me feel more secure going up the ladder of success, or because I like to acquire stuff; I'm just happy being who I am." She said, "Maybe some women might have to have a baby to feel secure, but I need to be busy and creative to feel secure. I like my title to read 'working woman,' not 'working mom.'" When I asked her if she ever regrets her decision to stay child-free, her answer was, "Not for more than five minutes."

Not long ago, I heard a childless woman comment that because she and her husband have had to be caregivers for both of their parents for so long, they can't imagine what it would have been like to care for children as well. Now they are free from both sets of parents and are looking forward to just enjoying each other and the good life, traveling and taking each day as it comes without any stresses or worries. They say they are so glad they never had children, because their lives would have to be focused on them—and likely grandchildren—instead of on each other.

Chapter 18
Women's Views

These are some of the personal stories that I have heard from friends, clients, and relatives over the past decade; I documented them in my journal. They are sometimes controversial, but I wanted to share them with other women who may or may not be in the same situation.

❧ ☙

Yuko, who was a twenty-eight-year-old Japanese girl visiting Canada on a holiday, had a different outlook on why she was without children—and one I found most interesting. When I asked her why she was against children, she said, "I'm afraid of the responsibility, and also of the commitment of having to care for someone else other than myself. I'm happy and very content. My mom really wants to be a grandma, and my dad's dream is to be a grandpa, and also to have someone work with him in our family grocery store. I will feel guilty if I don't give them that opportunity, but I don't want the responsibility of looking after a baby, because I feel as if I am still their baby."

❧ ☙

I met Carolyn in a night class about ten years ago while going to medical office school. While we studied for exams, she would start talking about her personal life. She was a divorced woman who had chosen not to have children. She had been busy in her life as an airline flight attendant until she was thirty-five years old, and she had the freedom to travel anywhere in the world she wanted. She said, "I resent people who criticize me for not having children. It's not because I was selfish, but I'm a free spirit—almost like a gypsy. My freedom and independence are all I ever dreamed of, so I wish people would just quit asking me why I don't want kids."

I asked her, "Don't you ever wish you had a child?"

She answered with, "I'm not mommy material ... I never was. Besides, you can't travel with kids."

I was sad when the course ended, because I looked forward to her laughter and enthusiastic outlook on life every week. On the night before the class did end, one of the girls asked her, "Where do you get all your energy and zest for life from?"

Her answer was simply, "I love life, and I love my life the way I've molded it."

We all passed our exams, and the last time I saw her was at graduation night, where she had everyone laughing and coming out of their shells. Her philosophy was, "If you let the word 'childless' get to you, it will."

This note came to me from a lovely woman by the name of Joanie, whom I met while I was having breakfast one morning at a local coffee shop.

> Regarding what others might say to me, because I am childless, I only respond with loving thoughts from my heart. I only want to do Gods will through me- so perhaps God's grace for me is through charity for children. I have a lot of love to give, and the ways are shown to me, I only have to open my heart. I know that my heartaches are my gifts.

Chapter 19
Not Having A Choice

We hear a lot about the women who made the choice to be childless and how wonderful a life it is for them. They can travel and spend all their money on whatever they want—or, if they don't have money, they can just be free from the commitment of children. We hear about how they basically are happy in this lifestyle.

But what about the sad stories of women who never had the choice—and who would have loved to have even one child? Not a whole lot of people ever give them a second thought.

In the following pages, you will read some of the testimonies of those very women who did not have the choice or the chance to become pregnant. As much as they would have loved to become a parent and raise a child, they were not fortunate enough to have that privilege.

These women were only too glad to share their true stories with me over the years. Most of them have since moved on and found happiness without children.

These stories shed light on women who were unfortunately not able to have a child of their own, but who wanted desperately to be biological mothers. Hopefully, their stories will show other involuntarily childless women just how many others share the same consequences and opinions.

One of my dearest friends says she doesn't like the way people judge her because she doesn't have kids. She said, "They seem to assume that I am a lesbian or have no sex life," she once told me and several other women. "I wish people would not judge me, because I never had the choice. I don't consider myself old, but I don't think having a child at my age—forty—would be a good choice now, either, because of the health risks for me or the baby."

The stigma attached to being childless and single at any age is very hurtful. The hurtful remarks are usually from women who are married and have a couple kids. Childless women don't judge women who have a bunch of kids and didn't want them, or a woman who gives birth to a baby that she says was an accident.

At a women's night out several years ago, one of the women expressed a very different view on the subject of being childless, She said, "What makes me mad about being childless is when your friends that had children, seem to alienate you." It's like you don't fit into their lifestyle if you don't know anything about teething, breast feeding, and diaper rash. It makes me feel unequal or inadequate. I wish I could change the way a lot of women feel about us women who don't have kids. The other thing I hate is when they put a baby right in your arms without considering your feelings; they don't ask or realize that maybe that is hurtful or inconsiderate. It wasn't my choice to be childless, but people don't seem to realize that. For some reason, everyone presumes that I didn't want them."

Another girl sitting nearby whom I didn't know, and who obviously had children or a child, piped up and said, I want to say something, She said, "I have something to say, and want everyone to listen." Everyone kept quiet to hear what she wanted to say. She said in a rather sad tone of voice, "Until this very minute, I never realized that aspect of a childless woman's life before. I feel terrible that I am guilty of that very thing: I always just presumed that women without children chose not to have them. In fact, quite often, I will put my baby in the arms of my friends who are childless, because I just thought it would make them feel good. But now I see it altogether differently, and I want to thank you for sharing and pointing that out to me. From now on, I will be careful with and more sensitive to women who don't have children." The room went silent after she made her speech; it felt as though the women in the room who had children were experiencing a life-changing moment.

This is an e-mail I received from a childless woman in California whom I had met several years ago. Her name is Angelina, and I like her story, because it relates to so many women who are childless by chance.

> I am forty one years old, and I feel like life has cheated me out of the best chapter of my entire life, my husband was killed in a motor cycle accident shortly after we were married, and I lost my baby I was carrying at five months. I have never ever found a man I would consider marrying again, and don't want to get married to any man, just because I want a child. My best years for delivering a baby are almost behind me, and if I don't find the right man soon I will go through life without a child, but I am a positive person, and if I have to live my life alone and without children, I will do so and make the best of it, but it certainly wouldn't have been my choice had my husband not got killed.

I have many involuntarily childless friends who say the worst thing they deal with is the continuous baby-shower invitation. When they walk into the room at a shower, only to see about nine or ten babies there, they feel intimidated, because they are the only one there who doesn't have a cute little baby or who isn't wearing a maternity smock. All the girls are talking only about what it was like to deliver a baby and how long they were in labor. As they pass the baby book around, they feel like immediately passing it right on by to the next person, because there is nothing more boring than looking at someone else's baby pictures. Quite often, not one person even asks how they are doing, because everyone is too wrapped up in talk about their babies. These types of situations arise all the time for the women who don't have children. If holding babies or being around babies bothers you, my suggestion is to avoid going to baby showers. You can always plan other things on the same day, and no one will ever know the difference.

This was a letter I received through the mail from a friend of a friend who, for obvious reasons, wanted to her story told.

> My husband and I have always loved kids, but couldn't conceive a child in the first ten years of our marriage, so had to unfortunately put the idea of kids to rest so that we could get on with our life. We once surrounded our self with other people's kids when we had time, but now as we are getting older, and find that we don't have the patience or the stamina we once had. We are fortunate in as much that we have grown closer because of having no children, but it wouldn't have been our choice to go through life with no children. My husband and I have had a super close relationship, we spoil each other and appreciate our quality time together. I'm sure if we had our own kids, we would be looking forward to the day when they leave home. Our life is happy and content and most of the time we say to our self, "maybe this is the good life and we don't even know it".

Chapter 20
Love Thy Family

I personally know at least twenty-five women who are childless at the present time. For some, it's by choice. Sadly, for the others, it was by chance.

I have heard both sides of this scenario, because throughout my life as a woman who couldn't conceive, I was always interested in the similar stories of women who were childless. I suppose these stories helped me feel that I wasn't alone; maybe they contributed to my therapy and healing process.

I don't know for sure, but I do know that whenever childless women get talking about what time of year we feel the most left out or lonely, we all agree that it is without a doubt the festive times, especially Christmas, when people who do have grown-up kids have the joy of them coming home for the occasion. You get invited, all right, because you're family, and you wouldn't dream of being anywhere else in most cases. But as much as everyone tries to make you feel at home, you still somehow feel as if something is missing.

I always point out to these women that they must cherish this quality time with their families just the same. I try to make them realize that they are so fortunate to be a part of any family, and I urge them to consider that a lot of women in our same situation might not have any siblings or friends to go to for the holidays. Think of how lonely those women must feel all the time—not just the festive times! My philosophy has always been, "Cherish and love thy family, because they are your gifts!"

Some of my dearest childless friends say the worst thing for them is not having anywhere to call home once their parents are gone; one woman says she feels somewhat like an orphan. Others say the worst thing is knowing that when they get old, there won't be anyone to care for them or anyone to come for a visit. That is why I feel these women have to have lives that are fulfilling and rewarding for them now; they must find happiness and contentment without having children. I encourage women to stay active and involved with the community by volunteering; you meet so many wonderful people, and it is very rewarding to give something back. Stay connected with friends and relatives and join outdoor activities or indoor sports, where you meet so many new people. Stay active and take up meditation, yoga, or tai chi for relaxation. Learn to pamper yourself with a massage, a manicure, a pedicure, and weekly hair appointments. Dine out with a loved one. Learn to love yourself. Get started with a new project. Be creative, positive, and optimistic, and always stay busy.

Every childless woman has different reasons for feeling alone or left out. The women who chose not to have children, although they don't have regrets, say the only thing that they do think about from time to time is being alone and old. We often talk about people we do know who had children who are not caring for their parents even when they are young, let alone old. So I feel that childless women must maintain very good relationships with our families, friends, relatives and acquaintances, because they are the ones who will be there for us, should we ever need their help

One of my friends said the hardest day of the year for her is Valentine's Day. When all the little kids are making valentines for their mothers, they make them with such love, and the most precious little innocent love notes are always attached and addressed to "Mom." It is so beautiful to see, but makes her feel very left out from that special greeting of love on that particular day. She never feels that sad at Christmas or any other time of year—only on

Valentine's Day. I talked her into making valentines for any little kids she knows, and sure enough, they brought her handmade ones from school in return. She was thrilled beyond words when she received her first one, and she has passed this gesture on to other women who dreaded Valentine's Day. It gives these women something to look forward to, so that they don't find Valentine's Day any harder than any other day.

The hardest day for most childless women is none other than Mother's Day, when everyone is receiving Mother's Day cards from their kids. I received a lovely card from someone on Mother's Day once that read, "For a special auntie, who is just like a mother." I still have that card, and I put it out every Mother's Day. Fortunately, I still have my own mother, whom I treasure dearly; no one can ever replace the bond a woman has with her mother, no matter what.

When we don't have children, we have the golden opportunity, if we want it, to be closer to our families and friends. I feel that not having had any children may have brought me somewhat closer to family, particularly my parents, because I was the only one who was without children. Childless women who are feeling lonely should spend as much quality time as they can with their families—especially their parents, if they are lucky enough to still have them. If not, they can spend time with their siblings, nieces, nephews, or grandparents. They will find that time with family not only soothes the soul, but takes your mind away from the fact that you are childless. You can appreciate the fact you have family to love, and make them feel as special and loved as they make you feel.

If your siblings live close by, invite them for lunch or dinner without waiting for a special occasion. It will make them feel special and appreciated for the things they do for you. For instance, if you have a new sister-in-law who is of a different nationality, perhaps you could find a recipe for that particular kind of food and go all out with a Martha Stewart–style table setting. When she comes for dinner, she will feel as if she really is special. Sometimes, small things that don't cost anything can make a difference in someone's life.

I spent many hours with nieces and nephews. I always had special bedtime stories for them—some of which I made up. Now those same nieces and nephews are married and have their own little children, and they tell their kids the same stories I told them. The bond between you and a child is made with as little or as much time as you are willing to put into it. It doesn't have to cost any money; it is just quality time. It always pays off in the end, because these kinds of memories are what those children will hold dearest to their hearts as they get older. They will pass your traditions down to their children, with the memories of you attached to them

Sometimes, women without kids have a lot more time and energy to spend thinking up things to do with the family. For instance, if your family lives hundreds of miles away, arrange to fly or drive out to see them—not just because you have holidays, but just because you want to see them. Set up a family reunion and try to get everyone involved in the plans, so they too can feel important.

Some families have different conflicts of interest, so you could try to get those family members who have been feuding for years to finally see eye-to-eye. See if you can help in any way by being the bridge between the two people and by hearing both sides of the story. Try to get them back on track, in case it was all a misunderstanding. Let them know you are there to listen, not to pass judgment. A lot of family disputes are over money issues from the past or even childhood jealousies; in most cases, both parties are just plain stubborn. When it comes right down to it, they both love each other, as most siblings do; they just need to be compassionate toward the other person and be willing to let go of anger, resentment, jealousy, control, and stubbornness, to name a few. You will feel so much better knowing that your family has a much closer bond—and that it may be because you took the time to listen, understand, and show compassion where it was so desperately needed.

For some people, the holidays are not always about happiness—especially for a childless woman. Instead of looking forward to celebrating the season with her family, she oftentimes just endures it by going through the motions. Her source of discomfort is not the gifts or the cost; it's usually the uneasy feelings between family members who have been feuding all year long and now find themselves sitting across from each other at the dinner table. It is very uncomfortable, strained, and—most of all—stressful. It's not always as easy to forget familial strife, and some people never do, but at least forgiveness can bring peace and joy. If you don't have children, it's a perfect opportunity to spend the extra time with family, helping them to forgive one another. They will appreciate the time you spend with them, and it will make you realize how much you're really loved and needed when they ask, "When are you coming back?"

When a woman doesn't have children, she can often feel terribly alienated by people with children. I have heard of such a scenario several times, but I believe that it isn't because they don't think you're knowledgeable or inadequate; they may just think that it will hurt your feelings if they push the baby in your face when you aren't able to have one yourself. However, if you want to be involved and included in a child's life, whether it is a niece, a nephew, or the child of a friend, all you have to do is babysit, spend time visiting, and show you are interested. Chances are, you will be more than welcome at any time. The bonus is that you become very connected to the child, and before you know it, you're a very big part of his or her life and the word "alienated" no longer applies to you.

When we truly love from our hearts, we love someone just because they are who they are. We don't love them because they need our love or because we need theirs, or just because they deserve our love. We certainly don't love them because it's our duty, because they are family, or because they have earned our love. We only truly love when we can love ourselves first and then give love away freely. We have to give our love freely to those around us whom we want to love. If we are fortunate enough to have a wonderful family and true friends, we are truly blessed. I once heard the saying, "If you have one true friend, you have more than your share."

Chapter 21
Unconditional Love

There are times when love asks us to make choices, but true love shouldn't limit, confine, or restrain us, as I once thought it did. Love should bring with it trust, respect, and freedom—freedom to allow the other person to freely make his or her own choices, to find his or her own path in life, learn his or her own lessons, and become who he or she is supposed to become. This is especially important when a woman who wants to have children finds herself in love with a man who tells her she had better not get pregnant, because he does not want kids. A choice has to be made by the woman being restrained from doing what she really wants to do. True love means always thinking of the other person's happiness and respecting them, as well as their wishes.

True love has no price tag, nor does it have any strings attached. It should always be given from the heart, and therefore it is unconditional. When we can believe inside our souls that we are complete, precious, whole, and valuable as human beings, then and only then can we be truly happy within ourselves and experience all that this life has to offer.

Having a husband or partner to love and cherish is one of the most rewarding experiences in life. And feeling loved and cherished by someone whom you love other than your parents is one of the most beautiful feelings in the world. When you have quality time with your partner, enjoy it to the fullest, because many people get so caught up in their busy lives, especially with children, that they can sometimes very easily forget why they even got together with their partner in the first place.

Setting the mood for romance when you don't have kids is so easy, say most of the women in our group of friends without kids. They set the stage for love that is simply romantic on a daily basis, because they have the freedom to do just that. Some they can enjoy what they call a happy hour as just the two of them sit at home, either by the pool or in front of the fireplace. Some enjoying the opportunity to hear what the other one's day was like at work; they might discuss the next day's events, and so on. Some enjoy a walk in the park, or on the beach; some just enjoy listening to what the other one has to say in the middle of the night, or over a cup of coffee in bed in the morning. This is a great way to show appreciation, respect, and love for your partner.

I discuss love in this book more than any other feeling, because love to me is by far the deepest emotion one can feel. Just because we don't have children doesn't mean we have any less of that emotion. We may or may not want kids, and we sometimes might wonder what we were sent to this earth for. Well, we were all sent here for a very good reason, and one of those reasons is that we all have a gift to share: love. We all need it, we all have it, and we all want it. We must recognize this gift, so that we can share it with the people we love, respect, and trust.

Some people are lucky enough to have more than one gift. Some haven't discovered their one gift yet. But those of us who have want to share our gift of love with everyone we meet. We feel loved when we are hugged, smiled at, and warmly told, "I love you." It seems these days, more and more people need and give these three things more freely than ever before. There was a time when you didn't see many people giving hugs so frequently, but nowadays, in these times of such stress and uncertainty, it is quite the normal thing to see a girl giving another girl a hug, or a man giving another man a hug. The expression "I love you" is heard in just about everybody's phone calls before they hang up, in every country and in every language. It's nice to see and hear how much the world is changing. When you hear the expression "Love is in the air," it really is.

Another aspect of love is that we all have to learn the importance of loving ourselves. Many of us get caught up in looking after everyone else, and we never think or do anything good for ourselves. We were not put here on this earth to take abuse or give it. When we learn to love ourselves first, then and only then can we love others.

Enjoy the love of your life, whatever it may be—your religion, a partner, your passion, a garden, a pet, or even your career—just as long as you are doing exactly what you always dreamed of doing to fulfill your life. Being happy, being healthy, and showing love for God and all mankind are the most important things in this life.

When a person learns to love naturally, honestly, unconditionally, willingly, freely, they have learned the most valuable lesson in life; this lesson will bestow the benefits of fulfillment, joy, health, and happiness on them forever.

Chapter 22
Finding Our Passion

If you are one of the women who never had a choice, and you want to feel needed or wanted, spend as much time as you can with younger people. Younger people will get you doing things that keep you fit and active. They get you into all kinds of things you wouldn't normally do, or ever imagined you would do. They are so full of life and energy that you won't have time to get bored, and before you know it, you will have a full plate, doing things you never even dreamed you could do—from mountain climbing, snorkeling, car racing, and skiing to going down a waterslide. There won't be an end to all they will get you doing.

Young people have endless energy, but the key is to stay fit, stay active, and—most of all—think positive. By thinking positive, you can achieve any goal you set your mind to and be happy while you're doing it. The nice thing about all this is that young people will learn so much from you, and you will feel needed, important, and special at the same time. The younger generation usually loves hearing all our wise and unbelievable stories. You will never be lonely if you become a big sister to any one of the hundreds of young children who need a shoulder to lean on.

Some of us women who don't have kids get the most enjoyment out of traveling, so we're gone for weeks at a time. We don't always feel the need to have a chaperone; we make friends with lots of new people from all over the world, and we get to travel to their country and have a guided tour when we do. We save all our money for these trips by working long, hard hours at the workplace, and we keep in touch with the gals who can travel with us. Most of us will agree that not having kids has allowed us to be free and have the time and money to enjoy a very luxurious lifestyle. It may not be for everyone, but I haven't met too many women in my lifetime who have said they are not having the time of their lives in their early and exciting retirement.

It seems that everyone manages life without children in such different ways. One gal in her sixties, whom I met at an art class a couple of years ago, said that she feels her best when she is the life of the party, no matter where she goes. If she is invited to a party where she knows the group, she will dress up in her clown outfit, which she designed especially for making people laugh. She has used this clown disguise to visit local hospitals and make sick people laugh, and she makes regular visits to senior-care homes and kindergartens. She believes that in order to be happy in this life, you have to make your own happiness, and she feels that heaven is right here on earth.

I learned at a very early age that if you want anything in this life, you have to work for it, believe in it, and have faith in the Lord. Believing in myself and listening to my intuitive mind (or inner voice, as some people say) have helped me with my own problems, along with hundreds of other people's problems as well. I have always had a sense of humor, and it has helped me throughout my life to maneuver through some of the unexpected turns in the road.

When I started to realize that there was so much more in this life besides children, and realized how many hopes and dreams I had kept on the back burner, I decided to take some of those dreams from that back burner and just get going on them. The first one was a course in communication skills, where I learned from both the students and the woman teaching the class. I believe I learned more about life and people in those three months than I would have learned in a year in ordinary school. I was quite surprised at how many in the class were there because they wanted to get on with their lives. One of these women said that she was alone and had never had children; by the time the course was in its final month, I learned that she was one of the hundreds of women who had been very insecure about not having a child. She said that she hadn't started to feel more secure until she started to believe that she could do anything she wanted to do and began to think more positively, without regrets and negativity. She said that she kept hearing a little voice inside her telling her to start believing in herself, and once she did, she realized that her purpose was not to bear children, but rather to share her life with children. She was fulfilling her needs of love and giving back at the same time by getting involved with support groups and fund-raisers for Third World countries. She worked at children's hospitals as a volunteer in her free time, and she believed that her purpose was to give her love to children who were underprivileged or handicapped.

 I have read that it is more common for couples to have children without thought than it is for people to spend a lot of time soul searching and decide not to bring children into the world, because they want to live their lives child-free. We feel as childless women that we are judged by the women that have children, and we feel alienated a lot of the time, because we don't seem to speak the same language as the women who have kids. While we are talking about our travels with partners or friends and our shopping trips to Paris, the new moms are talking about their babies having just learned the alphabet or how to tie shoes. We are in a different category for sure, but our only hope is that someday, when all those kids grow up and leave home, those parents will have someone to talk to about their empty-nest syndrome. Then and only then will they see how wonderful it is to be free from kids.

 I have discovered through so many years of talking and interviewing women that the majority of childless women are filling their lives with so many other things that they don't have time to be regretful or lonely. They don't feel sorry for themselves, and they never seem to be held back in any way. A lot of these women say they have found their passion in life because they had more time to spend soul-searching; they have awakened to their true selves because they *didn't* have children. They have become stronger, more powerful as human beings, and far more spiritual than they ever imagined, because they have discovered who they are. The most important thing is that they are happy and have found all the love they could ever desire; they have what they call "the best of everything." The majority of women who are childless today say that if they had to live their lives over again, they wouldn't change anything.

Chapter 23
Believing In Yourself

We often will hear about women in their late thirties and forties who couldn't have children, but felt too young to sit around and mope about it, so they went back to school, finished their education, went on to university, got their master's degrees, and then found themselves teaching school— something they had always wanted to do. I love hearing those kinds of stories and encourage anyone to go for it, no matter what their age or status. If your passion is teaching school, oil painting, or flying an airplane, just go do it! If you think positively about your life and about your dream, miraculous things begin to happen. Visualization works wonders, but so does believing in yourself.

In order to believe in yourself, you have to also love yourself. As odd as that may sound, it does not mean that you are conceited or vain in any way. It simply means that no matter how bad things may look or feel, and no matter how disappointed you become over the unexpected things that happen to you, you still love yourself. If you aren't sure where you are going or why your life is in a crisis, believe in yourself—and then learn to love yourself. The benefits are huge, and we all can get there if we try.

Once you begin to believe in and love yourself, you will find so many more things in your life that are beautiful, rewarding, and worthwhile. You won't always have to try to find your true purpose, because as you traverse your path, it will be standing right in front of you.

Because my friends and I didn't have to plan our lives all around children or be a part of a child's life in any way, we could dedicate much more time, desire, and fascination to finding ourselves and exploring our lives in order to see what our true life's purpose was all about. Fortunately, on our journey, we met the most incredible and fascinating individuals who taught us more about life than any child or library ever could. The nicest thing about it is, we didn't have to wait until we were in our senior years, or until any children were all grown up, to experience empty-nest syndrome. We are all remarkable women who have found our own happiness, purpose, and inner peace; we have also found ourselves. I feel that many childless women are happier now than they ever were before discovering that they were unable to have children, because they have found they didn't have to become a mother in order to find their true purpose.

My way of thinking is that if you can't change a situation, you should make the most of it, no matter what it is, and appreciate and accept the things in life that the good Lord did give you, rather than what you may think He didn't give to you. I thank Him for my sight, which allows me see the beautiful flowers, trees, sky, ocean, animals, moon, and stars that I so often took for granted until my father lost his sight and could no longer see all these things. I thank God every day for my hearing, so that I might enjoy the lovely birdsong; my limbs, which allow me to walk in the garden; my brain, which tells me how happy I am; all my organs, which are healthy and allow me to enjoy good food when I'm hungry; and any other senses or attributes that I sometimes take for granted. I find that by always starting my day by thanking God for waking up in the morning with the sign of the cross, and by meditating for five minutes before getting out of bed, I can be ready to face the new day with joy and hope, no matter what unfolds in front of me.

Every day can be a day closer to reaching your goal, if you put your mind to it. By being positive and using easy visualization techniques, you will attract the very things into your life that you thought were impossible before. If you have a natural tendency to be artistic, musical, creative, or inventive, get out there and do something about it. You will amaze yourself with how much talent and ability you have hidden away. These gifts are just bursting to come out! Along the way, the friends you will meet will be innumerous. Believing in yourself will bring out the best in you and bring you closer to making all your dreams come true.

I met a woman not long ago named Kathy, who had made the choice not to have kids; unfortunately, she was riddled with guilt because of it. She wondered whether this guilt was a natural feeling until her inner voice told her to be a photographer for children. So she saved up all her money for a good camera, bought some props for background use, and set up her own business in her home. Getting to spend all day with cute little kids was a dream come true; however, she also got a firsthand look at what a responsibility kids really were. By the end of the day, she was glad they were going home with their mother. She said that more than once during her two years as a photographer, she felt confident that she had indeed made the right choice not to have any kids, because when she got to work with little children all day long, even ones who were all dressed up and so cute, she could see how much those children depended on their mothers. Kathy had not only found her passion, but she had also gotten rid of her guilt.

One of my acquaintances was a very attractive, happy, and free-spirited woman who said she had been struggling with the feelings of guilt for not having kids; she had decided not to have children at the age of thirty-four. She was a very successful and very well-adjusted businesswoman who was content and happy. She loved children to a certain degree, but for some reason, she just couldn't see herself as a mom. She decided to travel the world instead, and while she was traveling, she found her passion in wanting to work in hospitals in countries where the people were poor, undernourished, and in poor health. She said her biggest complaint with people is that they often indicate that she is selfish. She is still haunted occasionally by guilt for not having at least one child, but now, in her forties; she believes she wasn't meant to have kids in this life. Her only children are the kids she looks after in Third World countries. She said she recommends fostering children to anyone wanting to feel needed.

Chapter 24
Overcoming Criticism

Don't be afraid of criticism, for that is where we learn the truth.

"Why don't you have kids? Don't you ever wish you had kids?" These are such simple questions, but to a childless woman, they can sometimes be very hurtful. Many times, we have to turn a deaf ear toward certain people who question our childlessness. Sometimes, I feel like responding with an equally hurtful question, but I always bite my tongue instead, because I don't like to get into an argument just for the sake of getting even. I have often become the target of hurtful remarks as a result of not having children; I just brush it off as a jealousy thing.

I have a very dear friend that ever so often will say, "I bet you sure wish you had kids, now that you're getting older." Other childless women say they often encounter a statement that I feel is a put-down: "I would invite you to the party, but there will be kids, so if you don't like them, you wouldn't feel comfortable." Others say, "You should have had kids, because you would have been such a good mom," or "I bet if you had had kids, they would have been beautiful," or "Don't you ever wonder what your kids would have looked like?" Most of these comments have been heard many times by childless women, and most often, they are ignored or overlooked.

I talk to many women who could not have children for their own personal reasons, and because they are very career-oriented and are doing so well in life, they get criticized for having no children. One very inconsiderate and rude sentiment is quite commonly directed at childless women when a person they hardly know will comment, either to their faces or to someone else behind their backs, that they are selfish. I can't believe people are really uncaring enough to make such a statement about or to someone they hardly know—or, worse still, someone they know very well. Some people will even make a comment like that before knowing the real reason the woman is without children. Many childless women ignore the comments by pretending they never heard them in the first place or by changing the subject to something the other person has to address. I believe the "selfish" comment is one of the worst remarks someone can make, especially if the woman in question is childless for health reasons and had always wanted a child.

One of the hardest things a childless woman endures, is the sarcasm that is very often thrown out to them, like, "It must be nice blowing all your money on yourself." Even if the most giving and generous childless women will be targeted by such comments; their virtue seems to make no difference. I tell these women to say something like this in response: "Well, actually, it's really nice, because I get to spend a lot of my money on the homeless, on women's shelters, and on the needy children of the world. It gives me a satisfaction that most people will never know." This seems to work every time, and you will likely never hear them say anything like that again; instead, they will take an interest in finding out just what institution you are donating to. Hopefully, they will donate to your cause as well.

I talked to one woman who said her relatives were her worst critics and were always asking personal questions about her womanhood. The questions and comments were both humiliating and out-and-out rude; one of them was, "You have to make love in order to procreate, you know." This was presented as a joke, of course, as if she could really be expected to join in the laughter, much less give them what they all obviously wanted, which was the real reason that she didn't get pregnant. She would feel exploited, humiliated, and upset beyond words. She said the only way she learned to make them realize how rude they were was to give them an answer that might keep them quiet, and that answer was plain and simple: "It's none of anyone's business." She says those same words to anyone ignorant enough to ask those personal questions. Depending on the situation and who is asking the questions, she sometimes will add, "Why did you have kids?"

My stylist, who is young and contemplating not having children, says her clients come right out and ask her, "Are you pregnant yet?" She is always so baffled at the personal questions regarding pregnancy, that she usually just answers with, "No, I'm just fat." The other person usually feels so embarrassed that they are at a loss for words.

I liked the answer that one woman of about thirty-five years old gave. She had a steady boyfriend of five years, and she happened to be very happy with her life without children. She said that whenever people asked her the very personal question of why she didn't have kids, she just answered them with a question of her own: "Why do you want to know?"

I've been asked some other questions over the years that I felt at the time were very personal and rude, to say the least. Some would ask, "Is your husband the reason you never had kids?" When I would ask them what they meant, they said, "Well, a lot of times, a man is impotent, or has a low sperm count, or just doesn't want to be a father …" I usually stopped them right in their tracks and told them, "It's nothing to do with my husband or his manhood, or me and my womanhood. I am without children because I chose life over kids." I usually got silence in response, along with a very dumbfounded look.

My husband and I attended a wedding once in Hawaii, and as beautiful and elaborate as the ceremony was, a lot of the guests were ignorant when it came to people's feelings. As the photographer took pictures of the beautiful bride and groom, one of the attendants came up to us and said, "So where are your kids?" We smiled and said, "Oh, we don't have children." The answer to that was "Why not? You don't know what you're missing! This beautiful ceremony wouldn't be happening if it weren't for kids, so you guys should reconsider." And off this guy went, as though he were some sort of an expert on having kids. We looked at each other and shook our heads, saying "Aren't some people ignorant?" A woman sitting at our table leaned over close enough for us to hear her say, "You don't know how happy it makes you feel when you see your children walk down the aisle; it's a feeling that people without children will never experience." These thoughtless comments are hurtful to many women who are trying to have kids and can't. Maybe someday, people will realize that not everyone chose not to have kids!

Once I got past feeling hurt over the criticism, I knew nothing else could or would bother me. I don't let any kind of negative thoughts or words get to me anymore. I have learned to brush it off my shoulders like dust; that way, negative people and negative comments won't mar my positive outlook on life. I love people and I love life, but sometimes, we must disregard certain people or certain words if we want to live healthy and happy lives.

Chapter 25
Laughter: Still The Best Medicine

Don't always think the worst and expect the best.
Expect the worst, and be happy with the rest.

One of my favorite memories from one of my nephews, and one that always makes me laugh, happened when he was about eight years old. We were driving to the park one day, and out of the blue, he said, "Auntie, why don't you have any kids?"
Surprised to hear his question, I answered with, "Well, I just couldn't get any."

His look of disbelief was intriguing, as well as surprising. He answered with, "But how come there weren't any more babies when you went? Because when my mom went to get hers, she got me and Trisha. So how come there weren't any left when you went to get some?" Then, before I could even think of what to say, he said, "Well, maybe if you go back again, there will be some for you, Auntie."

I was so amazed at how sweet and innocent a young child really is, I wasn't about to give him the story of the birds and the bees. But I still to this day laugh about it. I will likely regale his wedding guests with it one day, because I'm sure it will bring laughter to everyone.

One of my friends got the laugh of her life from her six-year-old granddaughter, who was asking her how babies were made.

Her grandma tried hard to explain that it was from an egg that every girl is born with; when that girl gets married, she and her husband can make a baby, because the egg will get fertilized, and so on. Well, a few days after this talk, the granddaughter came running into the house after playing outside with friends, crying because someone had bumped into her stomach. She was so upset, crying and saying, "Grandma, I think my eggs must have got broken, because my friend ran into me. Now I won't be able to have any kids when I grow up!" My other friends and I laughed and laughed when we heard this story, and every time I tell it to someone, they laugh until tears run down their faces.

Laughter truly is still the best way to relieve stress and worry. Laughter has a healing energy that most of us don't get enough of. It is easy to get caught up in the fast pace of life today; everyone is in a hurry, and they are too busy running around to keep appointments and schedules running smoothly. But laughter is a medicine that is free, and we all can recharge the batteries of our spirits if we just take the time to tell a funny little story. A good, clean, funny joke is also good anytime. Even seeing the humor in a bad situation can make a person feel good; it can be better to laugh about bad news than to be so serious about everything. I believe that laughter should be a mandatory practice at every workplace before work starts in the morning; it would help people have a much happier and lighter day. Try to make someone laugh every day, and the world will be a better place.

Once, during my first years of styling hair, I turned a women's hair green by mistake. When I ran out of perm papers, I used green toilet paper to wind a perm. I didn't know what to do when I took the rods out and saw that her hair was bright green. I could have lost my job over it, but I just laughed and told the lady that she was all ready for Christmas. She didn't see the humor, and by then, I couldn't either. I still laugh about it today, because it was definitely my most embarrassing moment ever. But I still could laugh, and when I had to phone the Crown Zellarback paper company to find out what chemicals they used in their toilet paper, they laughed even harder. I'm sure they laugh about it to this day, and that no one had ever done anything quite like that before—not with a perm, anyway.

Sometimes, we can get very bogged down with the everyday stresses of our life, thinking that our problems signify the end of the world, when what we really need is a diversion of some kind to take our mind off our troubles. Infertility can be both stressful and depressing, but it doesn't have to be. A great diversion should be none other than pure and simple laughter. We don't have to split our guts at everything we hear, but we really don't do enough of it anymore. Laughing is free, only takes a minute, and can bring a smile to the sick, sad, and depressed. Laughter can have all kinds of health benefits; it is the reason that Patch Adams's passion was to build a hospital where happiness was the foundation of wellness. If you haven't seen the movie, I suggest doing so. I have watched it at least ten times, not just for the humor but for the story itself—in which laughter has a healing power for everyone. It just confirms to me that we all need laughter in our daily lives in order to stay healthy and happy.

Make a point of watching funny movies and cartoons, rather than violent ones. Watch a comedy channel where you can find humor. The news isn't always happy; that's why it's news. It always comes on the television screen at dinner hour, which is when you should be eating your dinner, not feeling sad about the world. If we try to eliminate some of the depressing things from our daily lives, we can find a lot more to laugh about.

Keep in touch with any friends who are of a happy nature and funny at the best of times, because they can keep you laughing for days just by remembering what they said the last time you were with them. Laughter is a great way to get rid of your stress, and being childless doesn't have to be a sad thing. You can make it whatever you want to make it, so make it a happy experience; you will feel healthier, look younger, and suffer less stress. You can use this motto, as I did: "child-free and stress-free." It's all in what we make it.

I have made a habit of sending a childfree friend a funny card or e-mail for no reason at all, just to make her day—most of which get forwarded along to anyone who needs a good laugh. Laughter is truly the secret to feeling happier and healthier. Reader's Digest has always had a page in their magazine called "Laughter: the Best Medicine." I have submitted funny stories to that column, and I have laughed more from reading that page than from any other humorous article or comic book.

Chapter 26
Cherishing Our Friendships Like Children

*Open your heart and listen to others, for you
never know what you might learn.*

I believe that no matter how many things happen in your day, for better or worse, it is still a story, and someone else's story always seems worse than our own. I usually try to find the humor in anyone's story in order to brighten their day. Maybe it's just my way of getting through the day, or maybe it's another one of my great gifts—who knows. I do believe that our best lessons are learned from our own experiences and mistakes. If we wish to pass these insights on to people in the same situation, it usually prevents them from making the same mistake. For me, such sharing just seems to come naturally because I've made lots of mistakes in my life, and been through many trials and tribulations. Each time I learn one of life's lessons, I feel I must share it with others, so they too can benefit from the knowledge, and possibly reach their highest potential without all the unforeseen obstacles.

Having a lot of friends without children who get together on a regular basis for tea, coffee, a movie, or just a plain ordinary chin wag gives everyone something to look forward to. The topic of kids—or, rather, the lack of them—does come up almost every time we get together.

It is interesting to hear the different messages in our conversations that arise as the years go by and as we age gracefully. The conversational themes have changed considerably from "Poor me," to "Aren't we lucky that we didn't have kids?" to "Just think how lucky we are to be sitting here together as a close group of friends, for the last twenty years—think of how much we have grown and healed, and how much more confident we are without kids!" We see ourselves these days as much more healthy, complete, whole, happy, secure, enthusiastic, compassionate, balanced, spiritual, and most of all more loving as women.

We have learned to laugh at things that at one time you didn't dare laugh at. We compare notes and see humor in our daily lives that we would have missed a few years ago. We bring at least one funny story to the table every time we get together, so we all can laugh—sometimes so hard that tears run down our faces and our stomachs hurt the next day. We believe that the laughter in our lives has kept us all healthy over the years.

Having deep connections with friends should hold a higher priority than, or at least hold just as much priority as, being a mom, making more money, having a title, or looking more perfect for others. If women would focus on improving their relationships with friends, they would improve their quality of life, both spiritually and mentally; they would attract love, health, and happiness into their lives on a daily basis.

One thing is for sure: when you don't have children, you sure have a lot of quality time for friends. I seem to attract people of any age and status to my list of friends; I learned at a very young age that in order to make or have good friends, you have to be a good friend. I started to put those words into more and more practice as I got used to the idea that I was going to be childless. I would make a special point of asking new acquaintances when they were born; when they would tell me, I would intentionally remember it until I could write it in my birthday journal. When they received a card from me on their birthdays, they would be so surprised, and before I knew it, I would be receiving one from them, and I had also made more new friends. From that simple, fun gesture, I made some very dear and caring friends that I still have to this day. Sometimes a very small gesture can change a person's life forever.

I know that women without children work extra hard at maintaining good, long lasting relationships. I will share with you another approach that I have always thought of as being a sure way to make a good friend: be as caring for them as you would be for yourself. Ask them how they are doing. Ask questions about them and their families (but nothing too personal) instead of talking about yourself and where you are going. Asking questions is always a good way to let someone know you really do care about them as a person. Also, remember what they told you, so you can ask about that particular situation the next time you see them, in case they are still trying to cope. Chances are, they will be amazed that you remembered, and your thoughtfulness and caring personality is going to mean a lot to a new friend.

The ability to be a good listener to those around you, whether they are family members, friends, or acquaintances, is a huge asset, and something I've always considered a gift. Not everyone has the knack for listening; if you do, you will not only gain trust and respect, but you will also gain multitudes of very special and long-lasting friends. Many people are reluctant to get too close to others for fear of getting rejected or hurt. But if they learn to open up their hearts and believe in themselves, they will become healthier and happier individuals.

A deeper connection with friends should hold a higher priority than just being right, or having the best career, or having better looks than others. If we can focus on improving and deepening our relationships with friends by leaving all our feelings of despair, guilt, shame, regret, frustration, and resentment behind, our quality of life—both spiritual and mental—will only improve to the highest level of peace and happiness.

Some of the friends I have made since I have been without children, are as close as, or closer to me, than blood relatives.

This is because I was able to spend more time with them than I normally would have, had I had kids of my own to care for.

As we get older and feel our age creeping up on us, we find ourselves spending more and more time pampering ourselves, either with beautiful health spas or weekend retreats. We have more time to travel to places that once seemed unattainable. Now we can get on the computer, search for a destination, purchase plane tickets online, and be packed and gone by the next weekend. Many times, on these very trips, we find ourselves meeting more people who are in the same boat: they have no children, they are financially secure, they are sometimes bored, and they have time to travel anywhere they want. They want to spend the best years of their lives doing something they have always wanted to do; more often than not, that something is travel. Consequently, they are meeting the friends who will be in their lives forever. These types of trips can be both healing and refreshing, not only because of the friends you make, but because of what you learn from these people. It might just be as simple as the book they passed on to you, or the information they had on a health food that helps arthritis or a new doctor that is specializing in women's hormones. No one who crosses our paths—no matter the time, place, season or reason—does so by accident.

If we make the best of our childless freedom and realize that we really are fortunate to have the best of both worlds, we will find the fulfillment and happiness we are looking for around every corner. A number of women who found they had no purpose until they started volunteering are now more content and happy than ever before. They now preach to women who are feeling bored or purposeless to go out and make a difference in the world. Some of these women sponsor little children from Africa. These women continually raise money to send over to these children in order to provide health care, food, and clothing. They say the most rewarding thing about getting out and volunteering and staying active in the community is the friendships they make.

One woman I know has been buying shoes and clothing that are on sale after Christmas to bring to the very poor children in Brazil. She said that these children literally wait for her to arrive every year. Their open arms and happy little faces tell her that she is doing exactly what she was meant to be doing on this earth. She feels so needed and appreciated by these children, and she recommends this activity to anyone who wants to have children in his or her life in some way. The parents of these children become your friends, and they look forward to your visits every year, as would an old friend from home.

Another childless woman who is in her fifties, and who had been in our support group for a few years, said that she had mastered the knack of listening to other people's stories. Instead of always being the martyr, she would listen to their story and try to help them out in some small way. Before, she hadn't wanted to listen; she was too wrapped up in her own life and all of her problems. She was amazed at how much happier and healthier she became when she stopped talking about herself, dwelling in the past, and being so negative. She has made more lasting friendships than she ever could have imagined. She said that even her own siblings wanted to spend more time with her—something they had never ever done before, because they always felt she wasn't really interested in their lives.

If we make a point of showing love for our co-workers, our neighbors, our friends, our families, and even strangers on the street, we will begin to receive the inner peace, tranquility, and happiness in our lives that we all deserve. This love can be expressed simply by a friendly smile or a helping hand that opens a door for someone. Look into someone's eyes when you ask them, "How are you?" instead of rushing off before the person gets to answer. Show consideration and compassion. Listen to what others have to say. Showing this love takes little effort; why wouldn't you want to show it in your everyday life and make miracles just happen?

I feel that true friends are every bit as important as children, and they are worth their weight in gold. Treasure them always.

One of my dearest friends for over twenty years, who is also childless, and who is now fifty years of age, has come up with an excellent idea for women like us, who may spend our golden years alone. She said that we should all consider buying one big mansion by pooling our money and purchasing a home where we all can live as a big, happy family when we are faced with old age. We can buy a house on the ocean or on the lake; we will be able to have whatever we want, because the funds will be there—and, more important, so will our friends. I thought it was a marvelous idea, and I'm sure it will be a trend of the future someday for all women who are childless or for any women who have the money and don't want to live alone, without the comfort of company or friends. Such potential outcomes offer another reason why cherishing your friendships is what really matters.

Chapter 27
Romance Without Children

Take advantage of the fact that you don't have children and spend as much quality time with your partner as possible, if you have one. Call him during the day to see how his day is going. Make him feel as if he is the babe in your life, and spoil him as you would a child. It will make your partner feel special, and it will enhance your relationship in ways you never imagined. In return, you will both feel more deeply connected, and you will have more memories to share as your relationship progresses to old age.

Love letters have always been my thing; I like to write them, and I love receiving them even more. A romantic candlelight dinner or an evening dancing in the moonlight can also prove to be enjoyable. Be the instigator for planning romantic little trips away for the weekend, picnic lunches to a park or beach you've never been to before, and so forth. Outings together always prove to be somewhat romantic—and, most of all, relaxing and memorable.

Another romantic idea that many childless couples take advantage of is a date night one night a week where they relax, with no TVs, phones, or appointments. They give one another a foot or shoulder massage. They light the candles and dim the lights, pour the champagne, and have a nice, intimate bath together. The nice thing about this is that you become closer and have a much more intimate relationship in which both partners feel special, loved, and very responsive—and you didn't have to leave your home.

Spoiling your partner is a wonderful and natural habit to get into, especially when you don't have children. Remember birthdays and anniversaries and do special things together that are planned with love and consideration, as you did when you first got together. Make time for each other without feeling suffocated or joined at the hip, as some women say. Leaving a note for your loved one in his pocket before he goes off to work is another nice gesture that you have the time to do, since you're not up early to drive kids to school. Always offer one another a kiss before one of you goes out the door; you never know if it's the last. Never, ever go to bed mad about anything, no matter what it is. A goodnight kiss is a good practice, because you never know if it's the last time you will be alive to give them one. My sweetheart has always given me three kisses before going to sleep: one for faith, one for hope, and one for love.

Women of all ages are now sexier than they ever were; we have shops especially designed for women, so that we can look sexier than we ever thought we could or should be. It doesn't matter whether you are in your late thirties, forties, fifties, or sixties; there really is no age limit to being sexy or starting a new relationship. It's just a matter of taking the time to make your partner feel as good about himself as you do about yourself. A compliment goes a long way, and it's free.

Set the mood for romance on any given night with a quiet dinner in front of the fireplace, a drink of wine, and some nice music. You can dance to some of your favorite tunes; just imagine that you are on a tropical island somewhere. You don't have to spend thousands of dollars on a tropical holiday; you can have just as much romance right in your very own living room. If you like the idea of a nice romantic movie, so be it: make a big bowl of popcorn, dim the lights, and enjoy your own little private movie.

Chapter 28
Letting Go Of Fear

Do not allow fear to ruin the joy of what your life really can be.

The biggest hurdle for me to get over was that of fear. It was truly my enemy and seemed to hover over me with a vengeance, like a dark cloud. My fear was that I would be all alone when I got old. Who would be there with me? I had to sit down and realize that this fear was holding me back from moving forward. I had to face it head-on, realize it, analyze it, and deal with it. I had to visualize its energy and then let it go, just as one would let go of a helium balloon. It took lots of meditation, visualization, and prayer to eradicate my fears of being alone in old age. I found my own words of wisdom, which are, "No one knows for sure how long we are going to live, so why waste your life worrying about something that may never come to pass?" I live by these words, because they free me from being scared, fearful, hesitant, and critical of any emotions that transmit a negative energy.

Now I try to emphasize visualization to other childless women that are facing life without children and feeling fearful of old age. I tell them to visualize how many friends and relatives will be there for them, surrounding them with love, undivided attention, and support. I tell them to enjoy every minute of every day as though it were their last; they will be more content, happy, and healthy, and they will rid themselves of their fear of being alone in old age.

The biggest thing to remember is that we have all fallen once or twice, but we do get back on our feet, so do not give up. If at first you don't succeed in getting rid of your fear, try and try again. Don't keep visualizing negative memories or visions by playing them over and over in your mind; instead, replay a vision in your mind of your happiest memories, and keep moving forward. It is also important to avoid letting negative people influence you with negative opinions regarding your fears; that will steal your confidence and cause you to fall right back into your fear.

We all have had sad and unfortunate things happen to us at one time or another in our lives. We are sorry that they happened, but that doesn't mean that we have to give up all the beauty that is about to happen to us because of what we think might happen—or even because of what did happen.

Chapter 29
Letting Go Of Resentment

There was a time in my life when I resented so many people and so many things that I couldn't count them all. I resented my husband because I wasn't getting pregnant; if you can believe that. Looking back on it now, I can only laugh, thinking that it wasn't him whose biological clock ran out; it wasn't him who had cancer and had to have a hysterectomy; it wasn't him making me stay in a marriage that I wasn't happy in.

Once I became aware that resentment is like a poison that can hurt or damage everyone, not only myself, I was ready to accept that by letting the resentment go, I would be not only healing myself, but all the people I was hurting as well.

So instead of allowing resentment to fester and send out negative and hurtful energy to others, I decided to talk about it out loud, face it, acknowledge it, and just let it go. This is so much easier than carrying resentment around on your shoulders.

Whenever you start thinking resentful thoughts about anyone, just consider the harm you could be doing to those people— usually people you love or care about. Replace that resentment with a positive thought about the person you were resentful toward. Look at the situation as I did and see whether you still want to be resentful toward someone.

Even if you try to hide your resentments, refusing to speak of them aloud, they are still there, eating away at your soul and manifesting poison that can only hurt both of you. Just as much as we like clearing toxins from the air we breathe, we should also clean our souls of the poison of resentment.

When we harbor resentment, we hurt everyone; release it, and set your heart free. You will be so much happier and healthier, and you will have a new lease on life.

Chapter 30
Life Is What We Make It

Make money one of your goals, but not one of your loves.

Whenever I have the opportunity to ask my friends or clients what their ultimate dream life would be, they more often than not will say, "I just want a man to love, and to have money." They say they want to live in a big mansion or own a cottage on the ocean in Hawaii. They want to be able to golf all summer, not have to work, and spend as much money as they want. Many have even bigger dreams: they want to be movie stars, or have their own television shows, or they want to be able to travel the world and never worry about commitments. The list goes on and on.

As I sit and listen to these dreams, I realize one astonishing thing: none of these women have mentioned the word "kids," which makes it quite obvious that living the life of your dreams does not necessarily include having children.

In many instances, I hear of couples who are "footloose and fancy-free." I have a new name for this scenario: "footloose and child-free." These couples say that they have been living their dream for as many years as they have been married. In all these cases, they were child-free. They have established lifelong, meaningful relationships—as few as two or three, and as many as fifty—that they say worked out better for them, because they just had themselves to worry about.

When you don't have to save all your earnings for your children's college educations, cars, or weddings, you can usually afford to go shopping for a motor home or fly to your favorite getaway anytime and anywhere. The choices are endless. They say that raising a child from the time it is a baby until it leaves the nest costs somewhere around $700,000, so a person should be able to afford the best of everything for themselves if they never raised kids. I say start your own journey toward old age, by being healthy, positive, and happy. Then you can enjoy all the benefits of being child-free—not only in your retirement, but throughout your everyday life as well.

A lot of women who have been my clients over the years decided to put the idea of children on hold for awhile, until they got their careers off the ground. They found that while they were so busy working and waiting for Mr. Right to come along, they found themselves enjoying the best time of their lives. They had their careers, their homes, and lots of money; without even realizing it, they had become very content and set in their ways. They are healthy, happy, and whole, and they live with total freedom and leisure. They have become so content with who they are that they can't imagine changing it for anything—not even a child.

One of my friends was having her doubts about whether she should or could ever conceive a baby. She was turning forty years old and was already showing a few signs of menopause. Her biggest regret was that she hadn't done the opposite of what she did, which was to have a relationship, marriage, and a family, instead of friends, career, and extensive travel. Her age has never been a deterring factor, and she says that if the right man came along, she would still consider having just one baby.

Another woman I talked to told me she didn't even think of her biological clock running out, because she had always gotten the impression that you could just have a baby whenever you wanted, as long as you weren't over forty and were fertile. When she was in her mid-thirties, she naturally thought she still had lots of time. However, she was still looking for the right man to come along when she turned forty, so she decided to quit looking, and she jokingly said that if she really gets too lonely, she will get a nice dog.

Time after time, I hear from women from all walks of life about how their lives were affected by being childless, and most of them say that they were so involved with either their careers or their freedom that they never really gave children a second thought until it was too late. Some of them had psychological problems in the past but have now recovered from the stigma of being childless. Most of these women say they always wanted to have children, but they were too busy having careers, getting an education, traveling, or just plain having fun and living as a single person, with no responsibilities except themselves. By the time they wanted to start a family, they were either not in a relationship that was suitable, or their biological clock had stopped ticking, and having children was no longer an option. Now they say they are thankful that they never had children, because they are comfortable financially and can afford to travel anywhere they want, spending their retirement years around a palm tree instead of around grandchildren.

I have also talked to many young women who are at a turning point in their lives. They are contemplating having a child but don't know for sure whether they are making the right decision. Some are not with a man and want to find a man only to be a donor; others want to get into a relationship only to have a child. I encourage these young women to not let anything stop them. If they want a child, they should by all means have one. They shouldn't wait for a man to show up or for their biological clocks to run out, or they might find themselves middle-aged, single, alone, and regretful that they hadn't had children. I give them my blessing and tell them, "Life is what you make it."

In this modern day and age, with computers, cell phones, Blackberries, and iPods, it is all too easy to get caught up in the fast pace and vicious cycle, forgetting what we really want in this life. We must set a special time aside for ourselves every day and faithfully live by this commitment.

Your daily meditation does not have to be very long; it can last just five minutes. If you give yourself another five minutes to pray every day, you will also be able to start the day with a more positive outlook. A half hour of stretching and walking every day is also a good way to relieve stress, and it does wonders for your overall health. No matter how bleak life may look when you get up in the morning, it will usually end up seeming more meaningful than you had anticipated. If you get into the routine of simple meditation, prayer, and exercise, you will find a more healthy and meaningful life.

Chapter 31
A Greater Purpose In Life

Open your arms up to the universe, so the whole world can embrace you.

My quick way to relax and let go of stress is meditation. I just find a nice, quiet, comfortable place to sit that is free of interruptions. I close my eyes and breathe deeply, concentrating on inhaling and exhaling slowly and steadily through my nose. I bring all my awareness to my breathing. I clear my mind of everything, continuing to only focus on my breath for the duration of the meditation.

A five-minute meditation is like a catnap in the middle of the day; it is a simple, easy way to let go of a lot of the stress that we all tend to accumulate during the course of our everyday lives. It doesn't cost anything, and the rewards are very beneficial: meditation helps to lower your blood pressure, calm your frazzled nerves, and clear your mind.

Visualization offers another way to relax in the face of stress. I have been practicing this form of natural therapy for many decades, and I find it to be a natural sedative. In order to take advantage of this method, sit in a comfortable position in a serene and peaceful place; it can be your favorite beach, or the top of a mountain, or just your own living room, as long as it is free of distractions. Simply close your eyes and breathe gently, focusing on and visualizing a place where you have been that was happy and beautiful. Perhaps this place was the site of one of your most memorable times, or perhaps you have never been to this place, but always dreamed of going. Imagine that that you are there, whether on a repeat visit or for the first time. Visualize all the beautiful things that made it so memorable or appealing. Before you know it, you will wake up from this visualization dream and find that you are refreshed, relaxed, and energized. Somehow, your worries will have completely vanished or lost their importance. This form of therapy is quite often known to lower blood pressure in the same way that a family pet is known to have a calming effect on its owners.

Every morning, before I get out of bed and as soon as I open my eyes, I thank God that I have woken up to the gift of a new and precious day. I pray for protection for my family and myself, and I visualize myself inside a big, white bubble. I believe that the white bubble is for protection from any harm that might otherwise confront me. I am then ready to face the new day with a better outlook, a more positive attitude, and much more confidence.

I truly believe that everything in our lives happens for a reason. When we really want something badly, we will hope and pray for it, sometimes for years. When it never comes to pass, we begin to wonder why.

I remember something my dad once told me when I asked him why I hadn't gotten what I had been praying for every single night. He said, "Don't be sad—if God wanted you to have what you're wishing for, you would have it."

I looked at him and said, "What do you mean?"

He responded, "My dear angel, you must realize that with God, anything is possible. If you were meant to have it, you would have it."

I didn't ask any more questions, but I was still sad that I wasn't going to be getting what I prayed for—not then, anyway. I was only eight or nine years old, and it didn't really make any sense to me at the time. After all, I only wanted a new doll—one that walked. But as the years went by, and I learned more and more about the universe and how fate works, I stopped wishing for things. I would just think about what my father had said: if I were meant to have it, I would surely have it, and if I didn't get it, I wasn't supposed to have it in the first place.

A lot of times, I would wonder why God hadn't wanted me to have kids in this life. I would question this over and over, night after night. In the end, I would always hear my inner voice saying, "God has a greater purpose." I would also hear my father's words: "If you were meant to have it, you would have it."

My life has been very blessed with many gifts from God. My gift of being an intuitive woman with healing energy has helped so many people, both spiritually and mentally. This ability is truly my God-given gift that I know I was given instead of children. I have an incredible man in my life who has stood by me for over fourteen years; I have so many special friends who are like angels from heaven. I still have my mother, who is another gift, and I am grateful for all the time we can spend together—and also grateful that she has such good health at ninety years of age. I have very special siblings, nieces, nephews who mean the world to me. I have my own good health and my wonderful life, which is truly a gift; I sometimes take that gift for granted, but I know it is the greatest gift of all.

I have been sent messages from the universe to write this book, and when I first started to write, I didn't know what I was to write about. Once I started to listen to my inner voice, it led me to the right path. As I sit at my computer day after day, writing my manuscript, I hear messages loud and clear. My writing ability isn't one of my biggest assets, but I know it is enough to get my message across to those who need to read it. Every day I discover new gifts that I never knew I had—like the words of wisdom that come to me from the universe.

My wish for this book is that it may help all the women in the world who may have become a part of the childless phenomenon, who are sometimes challenged with depression, loneliness, regret, resentment, alienation, and ridicule, as well as the feelings of not being whole as a woman. I hope it helps those women who sometimes don't know quite how to respond to the stigma of childlessness; hopefully they will realize that they too have a greater purpose in their lives. I want to help them to believe in themselves—to reassure each and every one of them that they are worthy, significant, complete, and beautiful as they already are, and that they don't need to be a biological mom to have any of these qualities. I truly believe now that if God wanted any of us who are childless to be parents, we surely would have been. In this life, we must count all of our God-given gifts and thank God every day for what we do have.

Not too long ago, while in Vancouver for a business weekend, I was introduced to a woman who is clairvoyant and very spiritual. She meditated with her clients and had past-life regression gifts that seemed to be very legitimate and intriguing. I had a session with her, and as I was meditating, she told me that I had had nine children in a past life, and that they had been tragically burned in a fire. She told me that the reason I don't have kids in this life is to avoid going through the pain again. Instead, I was to enjoy children who were not mine, so that I could teach them some of my many gifts. She said that one of my children's names was Joshua—and, strangely enough, Josh is the name I had picked out for a boy, had I had a boy.

My inner voice always gave me names right out of the blue; sometimes I knew who they were, but quite often, I didn't have a clue whom the names were connected to. The name Janeah had come to me many years ago, and at the time, I was thinking of names for a baby girl. I thought that Janeah would be a nice girl's name, since I hadn't heard it before. Many years later, even after I had realized I would never have a daughter, the name kept popping into my head. I couldn't figure out why, because I no longer wanted names for a girl. One night, it suddenly dawned on me: I was to use the name for myself, not a child. I'm sure it must have been my name in a past life.

Chapter 32
Childless After A Loss

If you can bestow the gift of hope in one person's life, you have found your purpose.

We mustn't forget the women who have had children and lost them, either by death or through other circumstances beyond their control. Too often, I will hear horror stories of women who had children and had them taken away by authorities who felt that these children were not in a healthy household. Even though the mothers and fathers of these children loved them to pieces and cared for them as much as they were able, these parents still lost their children. Those women, who actually gave birth to children and lost them through no fault of their own, suffer a very deep and emotional loss; only a loving mother would know that kind of pain. My utmost love goes out to all of you women who have been there.

My heart always aches for the families of the children that have gone missing and are presumed dead. This agony must be like no other pain in the world. I pray that the mothers of these children can somehow find some peace in their hearts and believe that if their children have perished, they really are now walking with God as angels in heaven. It seems that God always chooses the beautiful, good souls to walk beside him in heaven. They are only gone in body; we can't see their smiles or hold their hands, but they are alive in spirit. If you feel their presence near you, talk to them, because they can hear you. Sometimes, when you least expect it, you will hear their voices, loud and clear. They usually have some message to deliver.

My father passed away at ninety-seven years old. One time after that, while I was doing dishes, I heard my dad say, "If you're looking for me, I'm just in the other room." It was so real that I went into the other room to see if he really was there. I believed from then on that our deceased loved ones are around us in spirit.

A client of mine who lost her only son in a motor-vehicle accident a few years ago, explained the pain of losing an only child. She would talk of how the hurt of losing her child when he was so young and beautiful had left her with an anger and depression that only parents who had suffered a similar loss would ever know. She explained how she couldn't find peace until she learned to forgive and know that her son didn't die in vain. She explained that the child she had loved and lost so tragically would live on in her memory forever, but that the anger at first was overwhelming. This anger, along with feelings of despair, loneliness, blame, and regret, had torn at her soul until she found forgiveness in your heart and learned to accept her loss, so that she could move forward, and her son could rest in peace.

The loss of a child at any age is a great one. My mother lost her second-oldest son when he was forty-nine years old. Although she had six more children, she felt as though he had been her only child. She regretted not spending more quality time with him, and she wished she had told him more often that she loved him. My heart goes out to all the women who have given birth to a child, loved them, and then lost them far too soon, for whatever reason .Children were not meant to leave this earth before their parents.

When women who have never had children hear these heartbreaking stories, we feel sorrow for the families, but we never have and never will know the extent of the heartbreak that these families suffer. I feel at times that maybe that is why I wasn't blessed with any children: perhaps I wouldn't be able to cope with the loss of my loved one. The pain of this kind of sorrow is one that we childless women will never know. However, our hearts go out to all those parents who have had to deal with the loss of a child.

Chapter 33
Awakening To Our Healing Powers

Most of us have healing energy, along with the ability to transmit that healing energy to others as well as ourselves. Most of us don't realize we have it, so we don't awaken to it. We can practice healing with our voices by talking to someone who needs someone to listen to them. This practice can be done right in our own living room. We can use our hands to give someone a massage for their sore muscles or tired back. We can laugh with someone who needs to be picked up in spirit. We can use our healing energy to lift someone's spirits by giving them a helping hand in doing a chore they might not be capable of doing. We can offer a warm meal to someone who is hungry. I would very often give a haircut to someone whom I felt needed a quick pick-me-up. We can do some meditation or yoga with those who need to relax, look after the little child for a tired mom, or make some cookies for an elderly neighbor.

We can incorporate our healing powers in the lives of others in many ways; we can do this just by being loving and kind. Energy healing is not limited to only those in the field of medicine. We are all healers, and we all have the power to transmit a flow of healing energy to those who need it, as well as ourselves at any time—no matter who we are or where we are. We just have to awaken to our higher selves and believe and trust in ourselves, so that we can live a healthier and happier life.

I believe that animals also have a healing power and energy that is unexplainable. I have heard many stories of people who have lowered their blood pressure simply by being in the company of their horse, dog, or cat. Many rest homes now have a cat or several cats roaming about for the benefit of the seniors. On certain days, an animal will visit the home, whether it is a little goat or a little lamb, because these animals are good therapy for the patrons. Pets have also been known to calm the soul; I believe they are healers of the mind and soul.

Chapter 34
Feeling Complete Without Children

Many childless women feel incomplete without having played the role of biological mother. I was one of these women for a very long time. I feel now that if we look inside ourselves and find the true essence of who we really are, we will feel our loving energy, vitality, and self-worth. We will find love, joy, spiritualism, hope, and optimism that we will transmit to others on the same path.

When you awaken, as I did, and learn to nurture yourself and grow to your higher self by believing and trusting yourself, you will then feel wholeness, love, joy, health, contentment, and inner peace. We can learn from all those women who cross our paths; who value their connections to other women; and who surround us with their love, wisdom, and joy. They seem to come to us as angels, and we learn the lessons we need to know from them. We learn from them that childless women do have the power, the wholeness, and the potential within us to make a difference in the world.

We learn from everyone on our path the importance of wholeness—the feeling of being complete. We also learn more and more about the many gifts that we didn't know we had. We learn to share these gifts of healing, sharing, and receiving. As we go through our journey without children, we feel more and more complete and whole, as if we are roses that are growing petals, one by one. We seem to blossom and thrive on all the nourishment and gentleness we receive from the entire world that surrounds us.

I often think of women as roses. They are beautiful; they are delicate; they are hand-picked; they are special; they are the wonders of the Creator and of the world; they need to be nourished and handled with care; and are all loved by everyone.

Chapter 35
Being Happy With Who We Are

> *Be who you are and say what you feel, because those who matter don't mind and those who mind don't matter.*
> —Dr. Seuss

Being happy with who you are tells the world that you have confidence, power, and pride. It tells the world that you are not afraid of what other people may say or think. You have love for yourself enough to express your brilliance to the world in ways no one else may see. You can come across like the shining star in the moonlight; for the real you needs to shine for the entire world to see. Express yourself with the many talents that you were born with, along with the ones you gained on your journey. Your many gifts and talents that you share along the path are all part of your shining light.

If you are happy with yourself—your loving, caring, honest, beautiful self—then never change that image for anyone; that is the real you. Whether it is for a job, a relationship, or a new image, if the you that you are projecting doesn't feel like you, take off the facade and go back to the real you. We have a tendency to judge people by what they are wearing or what we think we know about them.

If you are one of the millions of women who have chosen not to have children for your own personal reasons, stand tall and rise to the occasion, because your voice needs to be heard. We are all women of the universe; we are here for a reason, and having children is not the only reason women were brought into the world. Our happiness begins within ourselves; being happy with who we are is one of the greatest gifts of all, besides knowing and loving our Creator.

Chapter 36
Ten Secrets To Happiness Without Children

Believe in your inner voice. How many times have you said, "I knew I shouldn't have bought those stocks," "I knew I shouldn't have gone to that party," or "I knew it was going to end in a disaster"? You're not alone. We have all done this at one time or another, and we learn over time that the warning voice in our heads was our inner voice—our divine guidance. Some people feel certain that this voice comes from our guardian angels, who are trying to take us by the hand and lead us out of harm's way. If we learn to listen and trust that inner voice that we hear so clearly, we can benefit in more ways than one. This voice is the guiding, invisible force that resides inside each and every one of us. We have to take it seriously and trust the guidance we receive; the results are sometimes miraculous and very often prosperous.

Leave the past in the past. To live a happy, healthy, and positive life that moves forward, you should never dwell on negative aspects of your past. I hear a lot of women say they regret not having children for this reason or that; they say that they would do it all differently, if they had the chance. I believe that if they were meant to have a child, they would have had one. It does no good at all to keep beating yourself up over past decisions. You would not have grown to be the person you are if you had not done exactly what you did. If God had wanted you to do it differently back then, He would have taken you by the hand and guided you to another path.

Look for new opportunities. Look at each and every day as a golden opportunity to set another goal. The doors are always open to those who are searching. Do not be afraid of new challenges. Never underestimate your ability to achieve your goals. If one dream fails, dream another one—and always keep dreaming. No dream is ever too big. Look for the opportunity to meet happy and successful people. You will learn and grow from their spirits.

Embrace your spirituality. Spend time getting to know the universe, appreciating all its greatness. Learn to appreciate the little things that we often take for granted, like the thousands of birds that fly all around us. Have you ever picked up one of their feathers from the ground and looked at the beauty in it? Every single minute strand is so perfectly put in the right place! I wonder how many people have ever pressed a butterfly into a book just so they could look at the beauty of all the different, breathtaking colors. I look at trees and flowers and every blade of grass with a whole new perspective, because I am seeing it through my spiritual side, which is every bit as important as my physical or mental side.

Love unconditionally. When you can love willingly, naturally, openly, unconditionally, freely, and genuinely while also loving yourself, you will have mastered the greatest lesson. Your life will be more fulfilling, joyful, healthy, and happy than if you hadn't taken the time. You will never be alone, and you will experience what happiness is really all about.

Give away kindness. When we are kind and genuine about giving anything we have, no matter how small it may be, our generosity always comes back tenfold. It doesn't cost anything to ask how a person is doing or whether a person needs a hand with a chore. It can be as simple as phoning someone to ask how they are doing or sending a bunch of flowers from a corner store to brighten someone's day. When you look into someone's eyes and ask how they are doing, do you really want to know, or are you just making small talk? The next time you ask this question, wait for their answer before walking away. It will feel good to spread your kindness around to even the strangers on the street, instead of walking past them in oblivion. Give someone a friendly smile; it might make their day. Give someone a compliment; it goes a long way.

Thank God for what you have. I thank God every day for all of my gifts. Many of these gifts I thought everyone had; however, we all have different gifts. The gift of life is my greatest gift. I appreciate every day that I am here on this earth, enjoying the beauty and the love that is all around me. I also have the gifts of my good health, my body, my spirit, and my mind. If we can spend even five minutes of quiet time in prayer every day, it can make such a difference in our daily lives. It doesn't matter what religion you are; you can pray in the car, at home, on the beach, or anywhere else. God can hear our prayers from anywhere; the most important thing is that you pray. Praying will help all your fears and worries become less burdensome, and you will feel a heavy load lift from your shoulders.

Practice daily meditation. Use meditation to visualize yourself as free from all the hang-ups you suffer and the limiting labels you may have pinned on yourself. Free yourself from all the worries and obstacles that stand between you and the person you really need to be. Visualize yourself as being perfect Justas you are; you do not have to prove yourself to anyone. With meditation, you can go inside yourself and create your own miracles, discover your own purpose, and live a more meaningful life.

Establish meaningful relationships. Sometimes we get busy in our lives, and we forget the people who are closest to us: siblings, parents, cousins, nieces, nephews, and—last but certainly not least—our friends. We might have to weed a few of our friends out every now and then, but nevertheless, we still must remember our dear friends. Always remember that in order to have friends, you first have to be a friend. When you don't have children, your friends and family are your lifeline; cherish and honor them. If you have lost touch with some of your friends, reconnect with them. Nowadays, the Internet makes it easy to find someone, and they will be delighted that you cared enough to call them.

Learn to forgive yourself. Learning to forgive yourself is something most of us never think of doing. We find it easier sometimes just to put blame on someone else by saying, "It wasn't my fault." However, when we forgive ourselves for all our wrongdoing, no matter when or where these acts occurred or how big or small they were, we can then be free from the agony that holds us prisoner within our own souls. We can then and only then begin to heal from and grow from those experiences. We can then live a much happier, healthier, and more fulfilling life. We will also believe in prayer and miracles as we watch the miracles unfolding all around us in our daily lives.

Love your child-free life. I always thought that children were the answer to all my prayers—until I decided to identify what really makes women happy. Because I was privileged in my life to be a cosmetologist and an intuition specialist, I could interview and talk to women for over thirty years. I found out that children were really not what makes the world go around. I had to go through many trials and tribulations before discovering that, but all the hardships I endured unmasked gifts that I hadn't realized I had. I was able to grow, heal, and share my gifts with other women who needed my support and guidance.

I know that my mission in life is to continue to share and give hope to all the women who need help in any area of their lives, just as I have been doing for over three decades. Such hope remains for all women in the world, no matter how many hurdles they have to stumble over to get there. I believe that each and every one of you will triumph not in spite of those hurdles, but because of them. I wish you all the luck in the world.